professional
perspectives

Series Editor **Mike Burghall**

Talking Business in Class

Chris Sion

DELTA
PUBLISHING

Published by
DELTA PUBLISHING
39 Alexandra Road
Addlestone
Surrey KT15 2PQ

First published 2004

ISBN 1 900783 64 9

Edited by Catriona Watson-Brown
Designed by Christine Cox
Cover illustration by Phillip Burrows
Project managed by Chris Hartley
Printed by Halstan & Co., Amersham, Bucks., England

Author's acknowledgements
This book is for Martin Worth and Mike Lavery in recollection of the years we worked together at 3M.

Publisher's note
Soon after completing the manuscript of this book, Chris Sion died following a short illness. This book is dedicated to his memory in recognition of his contribution to the professions of teaching and writing.

Foreword

There comes a point when professionals learning English simply want to talk. They want to develop from structured activities and direct language input to talking about various aspects of their jobs and vocational backgrounds. Like other learners of English as a Foreign Language, students of Business English need a free stage in their classes in which they can relax, talk about their work, use input they have received without forcing it and then pursue this conversation wherever it leads.

Mastering the target language is a gradual process which continues until the students achieve whatever specific objectives they have set themselves. It is a succession of moments in which genuine communication, as opposed to formal, coursebook-styled exchanges, begins to take place. My intention is to sow the seeds for 'intuitive learning', spontaneous interaction, where finding the means to express oneself is an art rather than a science. However, my aim is not to disparage other more analytical approaches to teaching Business English, but to supplement them.

Here, the term 'Business English' should be interpreted widely as referring to 'English which is job-related'. The students' workplaces may be in small companies, multinational corporations, colleges, universities, hospitals or other non-profit organizations. The students may be more or less experienced, and may occupy a higher or lower position in their various hierarchies. Some of them may not be in employment at all.

Talking Business in Class sets out to lever Business English classes into natural conversation by promoting informal, student-centred, job-related exchanges. Many parts of the book focus on bridging the gap between the classroom and the outside world, so the topics of conversation are real and directly relevant to the students' interests. It is not a Business Studies coursebook.

The book is intended for professionals who need conversation as part of an ESP course, who want to talk about their occupation and work-related issues within the framework of a general conversation class, and who want a little general conversation practice to supplement their professional conversation skills. It attempts to give students the chance to engage in conversation about their work and job-related issues.

A large number of books and articles outline activities for language classes and leave it up to the teacher to spot the potential for adapting the ideas for specific teaching purposes. Here, by contrast, the material is intended for students of Business English in the first instance, although many activities can readily be adapted for use in general language classes.

I am convinced that *Talking Business in Class* will prove an invaluable resource for language teachers throughout the world. The material will enliven their classes by helping the students get over their inhibitions and enter the rather exciting domain of conversing and exchanging ideas in a new medium of expression.

Chris Sion

Contents

	Page
Introduction	6

Section 1: Mini-Activities
11

Learner Training A: Beyond the Classroom
Active English Checklist	16

Section 2: The World of Work
19
Where Will It End?	20
Business Trip Negotiation	22
Moonlighting	24
Shoulder to the Wheel	25
Service with a Smile	26
Joyce and Ingrid	28
AEAs: Abbreviations, Emoticons and Acronyms	30
Creative Combinations	32
It Takes Two	33

Learner Training B: Learning Improvement
Date with a Dictionary	34
Learning Sequences	35

Section 3: Me and My Job
36
Working Diagrams	37
The Heart of the Matter	38
My Work and I	39
Career Choices	40
Talking Shop	42
You and Your Image	44
What I'd Really Like to Know Is …	46
Job Analysis	47
Muddling through Meetings	48
Developing Small Talk	50

Learner Training C: Creative Revision 1
Remember to Forget to Remember	52
Memory Aids	53

Section 4: Bridging the Gap 54

My Territory 55

My Type of Word Processing 56

The Thief of Time 58

Points in Time 60

And Now for Something Completely Different 62

The Printed Word 63

Now That's What I Call Good Service! 64

Price Consciousness 66

Happy End 67

Learner Training D: Creative Revision 2

Marketing Vocabulary 68

Football Fantasy 69

Section 5: The Business of Thinking 70

A Little Logic 71

Contradictions 72

Paradoxes 73

Do You Believe in Ghosts? 74

Silence is Golden 75

Some of My Best Friends Are Extraterrestrials 76

What a Piece of Work! 78

Quotable Quotes 79

Mind Your Own Business! 80

Talking about Time 82

Learner Training E: Learning, Language and Identity

Split Personality 84

Personality Awareness 85

Section 6: Presentations 86

No Need to Be Nervous 87

Effective Presentations 88

Be Prepared 90

Portrait of the Group 92

Demonstrations 93

Reporting Back 94

Magic Potion 95

Series Information 96

Introduction

Talking Business in Class is a collection of conversation activities for business people learning foreign languages. The emphasis is on student-centred active learning for professionals.

The free stage of learning

There are so many materials available to the student of English today: coursebooks, reference books, workbooks, videos, CDs, CD-ROMs and the Internet. The choice is overwhelming. Nevertheless, no matter how valuable the sources selected, there comes a moment when the students just want to be themselves and talk. This is what I mean by the 'free stage' of a lesson.

My approach to conversation classes for professionals rests on the following assumptions, which, taken together, illustrate what I mean by the free stage in more detail:

- Students enjoy talking to each other about their jobs, their professional experience and work-related questions in general, and can learn a great deal from each other.

- Students appreciate doing tasks and activities that are directly related to the 'real world', although paradoxically, some simulations and creative fantasies can engage them quite profoundly too.

- Students benefit from an unstructured, flexible method to assist them over the hurdle of moving towards authentic communication. Traditional approaches might be well or less well implemented, but once the students have studied their grammar, learned their vocabulary and completed the exercises in their workbooks, the moment arrives when they simply need space for unstructured conversation.

Part and parcel of an effective language-learning process is to create the conditions in which students can relax and talk. They might need support from you or from fellow students; many will have high standards and want to 'get it right'; but the last thing they need is the inhibition created by having to worry consistently about the accuracy of every single word they utter. Of course, students need to be able to express their intentions clearly, but in my view this will be best achieved in the long term by helping them develop the confidence and feeling of well-being to function naturally in English at whatever level they might be.

Structure

The book contains six main sections: Mini-Activities, The World of Work, Me and My Job, Bridging the Gap, The Business of Thinking and Presentations. There are tips on how to use the mini-activities on page 11. General remarks on how to approach Sections 2–6 may be found later in this Introduction.

The sections mentioned above are supplemented by a number of Learner Training activities inserted between the sections. The underlying theory is that working explicitly on the 'meta-level' and focusing on how to learn is an effective strategy for improving the students' performance. It's worth students making it their business to reflect on *how* to learn, and most of these activities can be repeated as required as the students progress through a course.

The instructions for presenting the activities are clearly laid out, with references to time, level, language functions, materials needed, preparation before class and steps to follow in class. They also include a large number of examples. Many of the activities are supplemented by students' worksheets, which may be photocopied. In the case of the learner-training activities, the aims are also indicated.

Flexibility and experimentation

The times and the levels suggested are guidelines only and are not intended to be adhered to strictly. I should welcome it if you were to experiment with all aspects of the material. The process of re-thinking the ideas will bring them to life and will make them directly relevant to the specific situations of individual students.

Let's take an example. Have a look at 'Personality Awareness' (page 85), which requires the class to be split into speakers of different languages. In the case of a class with groups of Spanish, French, Japanese and German students, but with only one Arabic speaker, one Korean and a Finn, see if there is another common language these three students might know. Otherwise, improvise something for the minorities. Let them take on the roles of observers, or devise a completely different task for them.

Another instance calling for flexibility is if some students are out of work while an activity refers to 'the company you work for'. You will have to modify the activity for these students. Tell them to talk about past jobs they have had or part-time employment they might have had as teenagers. If neither of these are appropriate, suggest they talk about their parents' work, or that of anyone else they know. If none of these is suitable, tell them to work alongside other students who are employed. Don't be afraid to experiment to make an activity more viable for your students. 'Nothing ventured, nothing gained' applies as much in teaching as it does in business.

Common sense

Flexibility goes hand in hand with common sense. Consider 'And Now for Something Completely Different' (page 62). Although this activity doesn't specify anything directly about business, in practice Business English classes will naturally tend to use job-related examples. The realia they bring to class will often be samples from their own companies. They might bring in merchandising for their products or even the products themselves. Moreover, the websites they refer to may be connected with business, and the helpful hints may be based on professional experience. If the students don't think of using their own situation as a resource, it goes without saying that you should encourage them to do so.

Similarly, 'My Territory' (page 55) does not specify that if you haven't got suitable maps, you should print them out from the Internet, and that if you haven't got access to the Internet, you can manage by drawing a simple diagram.

Worksheets

A large number of the activities include a worksheet. These may be copied and used in class. Again, if you can't easily obtain copies, be resourceful. Dictate them (in summary form) or write the main points on the board. If you feel an activity which hasn't got a worksheet needs one, devise your own. Don't hesitate to adapt a worksheet to fit in more closely with your requirements.

Note that the students are not generally required to talk about *all* the points on a worksheet. Moreover, if there is a detail of particular interest to your class or to a number of individual students, draw their attention to it. In a student-centred approach, it is important that the participants are free to elaborate their discussions according to their interests.

Procedural hints and suggestions

The following teaching pointers apply to all the activities and should be incorporated into your lessons as appropriate.

● The activities can be greatly enriched by supplementing them with flashcards, postcards, photos, posters, video (or DVD) clips or pictures on the computer screen.

- Play background music to set the mood.

- Encourage the students to doodle as they work to activate the right side of the brain.

- When introducing a topic, you can brainstorm the associated vocabulary, present it yourself or elicit it from the class. In practice, these three methods invariably overlap.

- Suggest that students follow up topics discussed in class by looking them up on the Internet and then swapping and discussing useful websites in later lessons.

- Activities can be written up as a report or summary for a homework assignment.

- Conversations in class can be continued at home via e-mail or chatting on the Internet.

- When students report back on a task, you need to keep an eye on the clock. Having five groups of five reporting back on a two-minute step is quite different to having a class of twelve pairs reporting back on a half-hour discussion. Do you want to open up the discussion even further or close it down? Is there ample time to be filled or just enough time to ask the pairs to sum up their discussions in one sentence?

- It's often productive to lead into a topic from your own experience, but don't fall into the trap of basing the whole lesson on yourself.

- Always be tactful and diplomatic. Be aware of your students' cultures and differing social backgrounds. John might be proud his mum's a professor, but Mary might not be so proud her dad's a street sweeper.

Pairwork

Most of the activities call for the students to work in pairs (or small groups). 'Decentralised' teaching increases the amount of student talking time, fosters active student involvement, encourages the students to refer to their own experience, permits them to open up and talk in a way that is less threatening than it would be in front of the whole class, and promotes a relatively relaxed, democratic atmosphere in the classroom. However, some teachers feel it is not without its risks. It means giving up a large measure of control; students might be making errors with no one to correct them; and many students revert to their own language.

There is some truth in all these observations. My reply is that you should unobtrusively keep in touch with the class by circulating, noting errors, and giving personal attention and lots of encouragement. It is neither possible nor desirable to correct every single mistake, but you should be aware of the students' language level and needs. Whatever the drawbacks, pairwork provides invaluable practice in guiding the students to function independently, without your constant support on the one hand, and their well-intentioned but potentially inhibitory effect on the other.

Some students will invariably lapse into the mother tongue. Coaxing them back is an on-going process which can certainly be wearying, but their participation in English *will* increase, so don't despair. It might never reach one hundred per cent, but this does not invalidate the approach. Just as if you told your classes to listen to the BBC World Service radio broadcasts, although not all the students actually did so, it would be odd to draw the conclusion that you should never tell your classes to listen to English radio programmes because not everybody does.

As a final word on pairwork, make a point of regularly varying the composition of the pairs so that the students get to work with as wide a variety of partners as possible.

Active listening

Active listening is a well-known method of improving communication. The idea is to echo the speaker's ideas back to them as a check that you have got the gist of what they want to say. This gives the listener a task to perform in forcing them to consider carefully if they have got the message. At the same time, it lets the speaker know if the listener has understood.

I suggest you encourage the students to use this technique regularly, particularly where the subject matter is complex. Listening is a useful skill to develop, and active listening is ideally suited to adult, professional business students.

Turn-taking

Working effectively with professionals demands a businesslike approach from the teacher. Who should be called on first? There's a danger that it will all too often be the loudest students, the ones who sit at the front, and those whose names begin with A. It's natural for teachers to establish their own turn-taking pattern, but it's a good idea to vary it. Discuss the possibilities with the class, making sure that everyone gets a say. When you call on students to make their contributions, here are a few ideas to break those patterns:

- Around the class, starting at the front.

- Around the class, starting at the back.

- Alphabetically, based on surnames.

- Alphabetically, based on first names.

- From the youngest to the oldest.

- From the oldest to the youngest.

- Starting with the better students, so that the weaker students get more time.

- Starting with the weaker students, so they can get it out of the way and relax.

- Based on birthdays. Students born in January before those born in February.

- Students put up their hands or give a sign if they want to answer. But keep a careful eye on the less confident ones who might need encouragement to participate.

- Arrange the sequence in consultation with the class, but watch out for students who monopolise being asked first. Make sure there's some variation in the sequence and that it's fair.

- Randomly, for instance by drawing names from a hat or closing your eyes and picking students 'blind' from the attendance list.

Finishing-off activities

'Finishing-off' activities are an important step in teaching procedure. Discussion should not be allowed to simply peter out. No matter how challenging it is to get the students talking, in every lesson the time comes to draw the conversation to a close. This is the moment to let the students express their feelings about what they have been discussing, to take up anything you might have observed in their interaction, to ask for feedback and so on. Give yourself a pat on the back if they don't want to be interrupted, if they have spontaneously started talking about related issues, or if they leave the classroom after the lesson still talking about the topics you set them.

Here are ten suggestions for rounding off smoothly:

1 Recap the main points.

2 Ask the students to summarize their discussions.

3 Have the students give a final reaction to the topic in one word or sentence.

4 Ask if anyone was unable to express an idea and still needs help.

5 Vote on the most interesting contributions, and award gold, silver and bronze prizes.

6 Say (or have the students complete) 'In a word, we can conclude … but …'

7 Say 'Perhaps we never will resolve the issue, but we have to move on' or 'Time's up. That's it for today. But there's no need to stop talking about it after the class …'

8 Ask the students for their reactions to the topic and the way it was presented.

9 Set a written assignment based on the activity as homework.

10 Collect some of the vocabulary that came up and get the students to be imaginative and use it, for example in:
   – an e-mail
   – a company report
   – a brochure
   – a leaflet
   – a business letter
   – a memo
   – a label on a product
   – an advertisement
   – a notice
   – a phone message

Conclusion

Talking Business in Class sets out to cross the divide between the 'outside world' and formal classroom instruction. This is a reciprocal process: bringing the real world into the classroom on the one hand, and internalizing what has been learned in class so that it becomes a feature of the way the world is experienced by the students on the other.

In the hustle and bustle of the 21st century, time is a scarce commodity for professionals. As a result of advances in technology, the dividing line between work and leisure is becoming increasingly blurred. Students have to make it their business to find time for their English, no matter how pressured they are. But learning need not always be painful. The student-centred, authentic approach taken here will give learners the support they need to develop their communicative competence. They *will* gradually develop the confidence to interact comfortably in English. Fluency *will* start coming naturally, at whatever level of linguistic accuracy they have achieved.

The ultimate objective of the book is that both inside and outside the classroom, the target language will have become part of the students' personality. Ideally, it will have become so much a part of themselves that it simply won't leave them alone.

1

Mini-Activities

Sometimes a whole activity can be easily expressed in a couple of words. The mini-activities contain 100 such ideas. Develop them in your own way and in careful harmony with the needs and interests of your class. They may be used as activities in their own right to fill a substantial part of a lesson, combined with other mini-activities, or used as lead-ins to any other activity for which they are appropriate.

Practical pointers

It's not easy to give general instructions on presenting the minis because of their variety. Nevertheless, here are some suggestions to get you going:

- Plan the minis carefully into your lessons with regard to time, level and relevance.

- Keep a couple of minis up your sleeve for lessons in which you cover material quicker than expected.

- If necessary, set the topics in advance so that the students have time to think about them.

- Explain to the class why you've chosen a particular mini-activity.

- Brainstorm vocabulary associated with the topic.

- Lead in to the topic evocatively by referring to an aspect of it which is not related to it at first sight.

- Where relevant, ask who has personal experience of the subject.

- Offer a selection of several minis and let the students work in pairs and decide which ones they want to talk about.

- Stress that the minis are starting points, springboards to further (job-related) conversation.

While the students are talking in pairs, move around the class informally, joining the discussions, helping where necessary and noting points for future lessons.

To give an indication of how a couple of words can generate a great deal of conversation, consider a mini called 'Presents at work'. Discussion points such as the following can be elicited from the class or presented from the front:

- examples of presents given and received at work;

- difficulty of finding suitable gifts;

- ethics of giving and accepting gifts in business;

- cultural aspects;

- company policy;

- how to react when receiving an unwelcome gift.

Let the students work in pairs. No pair has to discuss all of these, each of which might lead on to a further set of talking points, just as an informal conversation in real life does. Keep an eye on things as the conversations develop. Ask the students sometimes to explain how one point led to the next. If necessary, set a time limit. Otherwise, use your professional judgement to decide when to draw the discussion to a close.

Mini-Activities

Here are 100 topics for students to talk about in business conversation classes. The first 20 are all directly related to the students' jobs:

1 Talk about your best and your worst experiences at work.

2 Talk about your strengths and weaknesses professionally.

3 Talk about your first day at work.

4 Talk about your last day at work.

5 Talk about how you came to be in your present job. Where did you find it? How did you apply for it? Can you remember the selection interview? What was your first day at work like?

6 If you could change three things about your job, ...

7 What was the first job you ever did?

8 What was the worst job you ever did?

9 If you could have a different job or profession, ...

10 The best boss you ever worked for.

11 What were the main turning points, landmarks or milestones in your professional development?

12 In your opinion, and in your experience, does it make any difference if you work for a man or for a woman?

13 Your career (or your job): past, present and future.

14 Last week at work.

15 Next week at work.

16 What training have you received since you started your present job?

17 What training do you feel you need in your present job?

18 Talk about a recent presentation or meeting you attended.

19 Typical presentations and meetings in your company.

20 What are the most important FAQs (frequently asked questions) about your job?

Activities 21–40 cover a wide range of business-related conversation material inviting the students to express an opinion on various topical questions. Some address the teacher, others the students.

21 Is it best for the economy today if I spend, save or invest my money? How would you recommend me to save my money? How should I invest it? What sort of return should I expect? Advise me.

22 Is doing business in general, and is each of the following aspects of doing business, an art or a science: making a profit; effective communication; clear decision-making; creative problem-solving; radical innovation; increasing sales; any other relevant topic?

23 Company cars: big, small or medium?

24 Women and work.

25 What is RSI (repetitive strain injury – so-called 'mouse arm')? What causes it, and what can you do about it?

26 Organizations should make their working environment as employee-friendly as possible. Maximum productivity depends upon a happy workforce.

27 The profit motive is a key factor in doing business. Do you agree with the following sayings: Money makes the world go round; Time is money; A fool and his money are soon parted; The best things in life are free; The love of money is the root of all evil?

28 It is impossible to be completely honest if you want to be successful in business.

29 Imagine you wanted to go to a concert for which the tickets cost £20.
Scenario A: On your way to the booking office, you discover you've lost a £20 note. Would you still buy the ticket?
Scenario B: You've bought the ticket, but sadly you lose it. Would you buy another one?
What is the difference between A and B? Is it

possible, and if so, is it desirable, to be completely hard-headed and rational in your business dealings?

30 'The only really effective training in the 21st century is "on-the-job" training.' Is this true?

31 What do you think of the idea that employees should be allowed to bring their domestic pets to work if this helps them be more productive?

32 'The trade unions are no longer relevant in defending employees' best interests.' True?

33 What are the most important personal qualities needed to succeed in business?

34 Globalization is a trend which will pass away in due course.

35 What do you think of the euro? Has it had any effect on your job? Do you think it would be a good idea to go even further and have one global currency?

36 How does the present economic climate in the United States affect the economy in your country?

37 What do you think about cloning human beings? Do you think it will be big business in the near future?

38 All jobs create a certain amount of stress. What causes stress in your job? What are the best ways to cope with stress – in general and in your job?

39 This is particularly for single parents or employees in family situations in which where both parents work: How can you combine a job with having a family? List and discuss the key points.

40 How important is competition, in business generally and in your line of work specifically?

Numbers 41–100 are miscellaneous business-related conversation topics, again sometimes addressing the students and sometimes the teacher.

41 The least reliable business contact you've ever had.

42 Your best learning experience in professional training.

43 Which person would you most like to model yourself on professionally?

44 The worst communicator you've ever come across.

45 Your favourite company.

46 The untidiest office you've ever seen.

47 The most efficient person you've ever met.

48 The worst-organized meeting you've ever been to.

49 Your favourite products. How brand-loyal are you?

50 List at least twelve things you didn't do at work yesterday.

51 Make a list of things you're going to do at work tomorrow using at least twelve different verbs (or twenty for advanced classes).

52 List as many things as possible that you would never do at work under any circumstances whatsoever.

53 How do you prefer to pay in various situations: credit cards, debit cards, cheques or cash?

54 Gaps in the market. Think up a new product or service that will make you rich.

55 Discuss the organizational culture of the company you work for.

56 Discuss the impact of e-mail on the way you work.

57 Tell the students to talk about the jobs that other people in their lives have or have had.

58 Suggest how your organization could save money and cut costs.

59 Tell the class to work in pairs and brainstorm as many job-related aspects of a company as they can in one minute, then discuss them as far as possible with reference to their own companies. For example, computer applications; job-selection interviews; apprentice training programmes; cost effectiveness; setting priorities; marketing strategies; profit margins.

60 Tell the students to make a list of about ten of their possessions. They should work in pairs and discuss: when and where they bought them; the price; why they chose the product in question; the sales approach in the shop; marketing; after-sales service; complaints; and so on.

61 Tell the class to see who can hold their breath the longest. Ready, steady, go! Use this to lead into a comparison of how the students keep fit. Then ask what their employers do at work to promote fitness and a healthy lifestyle for the employees. What facilities would the students like to have at work?

62 What is the best way to watch your weight? Do you know the calorie content of various foods? How careful are you about what you eat? Can you get healthy food in your company canteen?

63 Ask the students to bring in a couple of photos of their workplace, pass them round and answer questions.

64 Ask the students to bring short videos of their workplace to class as the stimulus for discussion of their jobs and the organizations they work for.

65 Ask the students to bring in brochures, products, components, items of merchandising or anything else connected with their jobs as the basis of conversation.

66 Ask pairs of students to discuss what they have (and have not) got in common with particular reference to their jobs.

67 Each student contributes a discussion topic in one or two words. For example, 'empowerment', 'out-sourcing', 'call centres' and so on. The students' task is to look up (a selection of) these topics on the Internet after class. They then swap the information they found about the topics and exchange useful websites at the next lesson.

68 The Internet: the students say what they use it for professionally, how it affects their working lives and what their favourite websites are. More specifically, they can also say what they last used the Internet for: banking; booking tickets; finding information; games; fun; listening to music; and so on.

69 Tell the students to write an advertisement for themselves promoting their ability to do their job.

70 Ask the students if they know Caesar's famous statement, 'Veni, vidi, vici' ('I came, I saw, I conquered'). Then ask the students to prepare three similar statements that hold: a) for themselves; b) for other people they know socially; c) for people they work with.

71 Ask the students if you can trust them. Can they keep a secret? How important is confidentiality in their line of work?

72 Tell the students to talk to each other about the keys on their key rings. Do they have any company keys? What things are kept under lock and key at work?

73 Tell the students to talk about their watches, rings, bracelets, necklaces and any other jewellery they might own. What do they *never* wear to work? What do they *only* wear to work? How significant are these objects in their working lives?

74 Tell the students to talk about the impact mobile phones have made on their working lives.

75 Get the students to talk about the hobbies they have had in different periods of their lives. What skills from their hobbies could they transfer to their professional lives?

76 Ask the students to draw three job-related symbols on large sheets of paper and then explain them to the class.

77 Computers at work: benefits, bugs and blessings.

78 Computer viruses: Where do they come from? Why do people design and disseminate them? What can you do about them? How well-protected are you and your organization?

79 At work and at home, on your computer and in general, do you hoard things? What do you keep? What do you dispose of or destroy? Do you find it easy to throw things out?

80 Tell the students to talk about the times they have been camping. What personal qualities are required for camping that are also relevant for business, for example discipline, independence, resourcefulness, resilience and flexibility?

81 Have any students done military training? What lessons learned in the military can they apply to their present employment?

82 Tell the students to talk about quality. What is 'quality' in their line of work?

83 Tell the students to talk about something pleasant and unexpected that happened to them at work, a nice surprise.

84 Talk about your driving test and how you learned to drive a car. How important is your car for your job?

85 In your country, can you tell which towns or regions people come from by the way they speak? Do regional accents and dialects affect the way people do business?

86 What do people say are the main stereotypes of different groups with supposedly different mentalities in your country? Would you recommend different approaches to doing business with these groups?

87 Talk about one problem you solved at work and another problem you haven't managed to solve yet.

88 The story of your working life.

89 Talk about a mistake you made at work.

90 Tell the story of a complaint you made about a product or service.

91 Tell the story of a complaint that was made to you in the course of your work.

92 Brainstorm the word 'work'. Then brainstorm each of the words and expressions that come up. Group them into categories and go on to discuss.

93 Bring several everyday products to class (you must know their price) and ask who knows what they cost. How price conscious are you? Do you know the prices of your competitors' products? Try and find out for next time.

94 The students each pick something they know something about, for example how to do a PowerPoint presentation, and then teach it to each other.

95 Draw up a list of people who've been in the news recently and then say whose careers you admire, who you'd like to work with and why.

96 Parties. Are you a 'party person'? Socially? Politically? Is this an important quality at work? In your organization, do introverts stand as good a chance as extroverts?

97 Have a student talk about their job for one minute. The others then prepare questions about the talk (for about five minutes) and then interview the student.

98 The most intelligent person you've ever worked with.

99 What do you think about the enlargement of the European Union? Are you in favour of a United States of Europe? Would this be beneficial or harmful to the company you work for?

100 Each student has to send another student an e-mail (or text message) asking three questions about their jobs.

Beyond the Classroom

Active English Checklist

> **Level:** All levels
>
> **Time:** 20 minutes + a later session of 20–30 minutes
>
> **Language Functions:** Reporting
>
> **Materials:** Copies of the worksheet
>
> **Aim:** To encourage the students to work on their English informally outside the classroom

In Class

1 Ask the students how they feel about the current state of their English and gradually steer the conversation towards a general discussion of how to make progress. Stress that restricting learning to the lessons isn't enough. Ask the class for a couple of suggestions on what they can do outside class, informally, to improve their English, in addition to doing any conventional homework you might set them.

2 Divide the class into pairs or small groups. Give the students five minutes to think up some more ideas, general or specific, for working on their English beyond the classroom.

3 Tell the students to report back. Write the examples up on the board, discussing them as you go.

4 Now tell the students to choose a couple of ideas from the list that they would agree to do before the next lesson. Tell them that you will check up on them and will be asking them to report back on what they have done.

5 In the next lesson, give out the worksheet containing the Checklist. Tell the students to mark what they did on the Checklist and report on how they got on. What did they find easy? What was more challenging? Are there any new ideas on the Checklist they would like to try? Point out to the students that many items can also be used as springboards to generate business-related conversation. For example, if a student says they have a list of useful vocabulary on a Post-It next to their phone at work, they could talk about the sorts of calls they have to deal with; or a student who has recently read a product description can tell their partner about it.

NOTE: The Checklist, or parts of it, may be referred to regularly as a discussion topic throughout the course.

Active English Checklist

**Tick the boxes where you can answer 'yes' to the following questions,
then discuss your answer with another student in your class.**

1 Have you recently read an English:

book? ☐

article? ☐

trade journal? ☐

instruction manual? ☐

product description? ☐

brochure? ☐

2 Have you:

watched any English television? ☐

watched an English video or DVD? ☐

seen a movie in English at the cinema? ☐

seen a play in English at the theatre? ☐

3 Have you stuck cards, slips of paper
or Post-It notes with useful vocabulary
around your home or workplace? ☐

4 a Is your radio alarm set so that
you wake up to an English radio
programme? ☐

b Have you listened to any other
English radio stations in the
last couple of weeks? ☐

5 Have you:

chatted to anyone in English in
a chat room on the Internet? ☐

used the Internet as a source of
reference for information at work? ☐

surfed any websites (in English)
for fun? ☐

6 Have you written any of the following in
English instead of your first language:

a report? ☐

a memo? ☐

a phone message? ☐

a text message? ☐

a fax? ☐

7 Have you:

corresponded with anybody in English
recently, either by e-mail or by
conventional mail? ☐

made any telephone calls in English? ☐

8 Have you made any lists in English, for
example 'things to do at work today'? ☐

9 Have you spoken English to any of your
colleagues or friends or relations who
normally speak your own language,
in order to practise? ☐

10 Have you tried talking to yourself
in English? ☐

Talking Business in Class © Chris Sion published by DELTA PUBLISHING

17

2

The World of Work

The activities included in this section provide a
wide range of lively, original conversational
perspectives for professionals to practise their
English. They include material reflecting business
aspects of progress in the modern world, job
selection and competition in the workplace, and
negotiating expenses after a business trip.

Where Will It End?

Level

    Intermediate to Advanced

Time

    45 minutes

Language Functions

    Reporting on the past; expressing conditions; predicting the future

Materials

    Copies of the worksheet

Before Class

    Tell the students to bring their mobile phones, calculators, palmtops or any other small, high-tech pieces of equipment they use at work to the next class.

In Class

1 Tell the students to mill around the classroom and show each other the electronic equipment they have brought to class (see above).

2 Divide the class into pairs and tell them to return to their seats and talk for a few minutes about their working lives before the 'computer age'.

3 Now ask the students around the class to report one or two specific examples of improvements that modern technology has made to their working lives. For example, Joe, an order-processing clerk, says that today 95% of the orders he deals with are e-mails or faxes. These written orders are much more reliable than the telephone orders he had to work with in the past. Jana, a service technician, says that when she started work in the 1980s, she had to call the office regularly from public phone boxes when she was on the road. Today, she uses her mobile phone.

4 Continue by asking whether there are also any disadvantages, and if so, what to do about them. For example, 'mouse arm' (RSI) is an occupational hazard that was unknown before the computer. You can take steps to minimize its effect by using ergonomic furniture and taking regular breaks. Or you can turn your mobile phone off if it causes too many interruptions during an important meeting.

5 Lead into the worksheet by saying that modern advances in technology have occurred so quickly that life in the 21st century is becoming like science fiction. What does the future hold? Where are the limits? Is anything possible? What are the business implications of technological developments?

6 Divide the class into pairs, give out the worksheet, and tell the students to work through it and then discuss it.

7 As an amusing way of finishing the lesson, get everyone to demonstrate their mobile phones' ring tones simultaneously.

Where Will It End?

Read these predictions and indicate whether you think they will come true in years to come. Then discuss your answers with your partner. Pay particular attention to the business dimension of the discussion points, for example the potential markets for the various inventions, the financial and technical aspects of these innovations, and how such inventions may affect your working life.

1 Video phones will be standard equipment in homes and offices within the next five years.
Agree ☐ **Disagree** ☐

2 Mobile video phones will be commonplace in 2006, and by 2010 will be as widespread as wristwatches are today.
Agree ☐ **Disagree** ☐

3 Mobile phones will be about the size of a matchbox.
Agree ☐ **Disagree** ☐

4 Calculators will be as thin as a postage stamp and will be disposable.
Agree ☐ **Disagree** ☐

5 Within the next ten years, there will be automated voice-navigation systems in all cars. You just state your destination in a loud, clear voice, and the car will immediately take you there on automatic pilot.
Agree ☐ **Disagree** ☐

6 Cars will be replaced by small helicopters. By the year 2050, the car will seem as old fashioned as a horse and cart today.
Agree ☐ **Disagree** ☐

7 Space travel will become commonplace. Companies will set up offices in distant galaxies, the mineral resources of the planets will be exploited, and people will spend their holidays on other planets.
Agree ☐ **Disagree** ☐

8 Everyone will soon have a small identity chip implanted under the skin so that passports, membership cards and credit cards become a thing of the past.
Agree ☐ **Disagree** ☐

9 Learning will be enabled directly from data bases via electrodes implanted into the brain.
Agree ☐ **Disagree** ☐

10 Laser beams directed at the appropriate learning centres of the brain will enable us to learn physical skills effortlessly.
Agree ☐ **Disagree** ☐

11 Television screens and computer monitors will use holographic technology to create high-resolution three-dimensional images.
Agree ☐ **Disagree** ☐

12 Television programmes will be available by typing in a number on the remote control and paying as you view. Similarly, movies, documentaries, music clips and so on will be available on your own TV screen at the touch of a couple of keys.
Agree ☐ **Disagree** ☐

13 The moon will be used for advertising. Special projectors will project company logos onto it, and advertising slogans will be legible with a telescope.
Agree ☐ **Disagree** ☐

14 Life expectancy will be about 200 years as a result of advances in medical science.
Agree ☐ **Disagree** ☐

15 Virtual-reality systems will replace a large number of face-to-face encounters at the workplace.
Agree ☐ **Disagree** ☐

Talking Business in Class © Chris Sion published by DELTA PUBLISHING

Business Trip Negotiation

Level
    Intermediate to Advanced

Time
    45–60 minutes

Language Functions
    Reporting; requesting; negotiating; asking and answering questions

Materials
    Copies of the worksheet

In Class

1 Tell the class you want them to talk about business trips for a few minutes. Ask the students to work in pairs or small groups and discuss when, where, why and how they go on business trips. What do they like and dislike about business trips? In the companies they work for, or have worked for in the past, what is the procedure for claiming travel expenses?

2 Elicit from the class the typical expenses one would have on a business trip and write them up on the board; for example, taxis, flights, trains, hotels, food, drinks, entertaining, gifts, telephone, laundry and so on.

3 Divide the class into pairs and give each student a copy of the worksheet. Tell them to imagine that each pair works for a successful company. The company recently sent them abroad for a fortnight and promised to pay all reasonable expenses. Naturally, they are not expected to stay in cheap guest houses and eat in snack bars. They should represent the company in a fitting style.

The pairs should discuss details of their expenses and fill them in on their worksheets. It is not necessary to spend money on every single item on the worksheet, but it is important that each pair of students should agree on the expenses incurred. The amounts on both worksheets of each pair should be the same. You need between ten and fifteen minutes for this step.

4 Tell the class you have bad news. The imaginary companies mentioned in Step 3 have fallen on hard times and cannot afford to be as generous as they promised to be. All expenses will have to be scrutinized carefully.

5 Tell each pair of students to work with another pair. One pair should play the role of company bookkeepers who have to check the travel expenses of the other pair. The bookkeepers' task is to query the expenses and try to reduce them. The other pair, who laid out the money, have to justify their expenses and try to convince the bookkeepers that the expenses are reasonable.

6 The pairs change roles: the travellers become the bookkeepers and the bookkeepers become the travellers who present the list of expenses they worked out in Step 3.

7 Finish the lesson with a general discussion of the activity. I usually ask: Who were the most extravagant travellers? And who were the toughest negotiators?

NOTE: An obvious follow-up is to have the students talk about the actual business trips they make in the course of their work.

Travel Expenses Claim Form

Name _____

Destination(s) _____

Dates: Departure _____ Return _____

Hotels _____ nights @ _____ = _____

_____ nights @ _____ = _____

_____ nights @ _____ = _____

Food _____ breakfasts @ _____ = _____

_____ lunches @ _____ = _____

_____ dinners @ _____ = _____

- Taxis   = _____
- Flights   = _____
- Other public transport
  (buses, trams,
  trains)   = _____
- Entertainment
  of important
  business contacts = _____

- Gifts   = _____
- Telephone   = _____
- Newspapers   = _____
- Laundry   = _____
- Tips   = _____

TOTAL =

Moonlighting

Level
Intermediate to Advanced

Time
30–45 minutes

Language Functions
Expressing approval and disapproval;
speculating; reporting

In Class

1 Ask the students if anyone knows what
'moonlighting' is. Explain that the sense you want
to discuss is that of working illegally, without
paying tax and/or without a work permit. This
means what in many countries would be known
as 'working black'. The situations you want to
talk about range from doing odd jobs to being in
full-time employment.

2 Prepare a list of discussion points relating to
moonlighting on the board. Elicit ideas from the
students to add to the following:

- Is moonlighting good or bad?

- What are the consequences for the economy?

- Have you ever moonlighted?

- Would you ever moonlight?

- Do you know anyone who has (or does)?

- Would you be prepared to employ someone
  who was moonlighting?

- Would you betray a person you knew to be
  moonlighting by reporting them to the
  authorities?

3 Tell the students to work in pairs or small groups
and discuss the points listed in Step 2.

4 Finish off by letting the students report back to the
whole class on the most interesting aspects of
their discussions.

NOTE: Be sure to treat this subject carefully. While it
may be a perfectly innocent topic for some students,
others may be reluctant to talk about an area in which
they have to admit to having been dishonest or where
they are even working illegally and breaking the law
at the moment.

Shoulder to the Wheel

Level

Intermediate

Time

30 minutes

Language Functions

Making suggestions; expressing conditions and consequences

In Class

1 Introduce the idea of the wheel as probably the most ingenious invention of all time.

2 Ask the class to think of as many things as they can which use wheels; for example, cars, bikes, tractors, gearboxes, electric razors, fax machines, pulleys, aeroplanes, food processors, propellers, electric drills, wheelbarrows, lawnmowers and so on.

3 Divide the class into pairs and tell the students to think back to the invention of the wheel. The pairs should write a two-line dialogue between two prehistoric cave dwellers. One has seen the potential of the wheel. The other reacts either positively, patronisingly or negatively, for example:

A: Look what I've made! It's going to change the world!

B: That's brilliant! You could use that in dozens of different things.

C: I've just had the most brilliant idea. Look, it works like this …

D: Yes, dear. That's very clever. Now, could you go out and kill something for dinner, please.

E: I've just had a brainwave. I've invented the wheel!

F: I don't see the point. It just goes round and round. Why don't you think of something practical for a change?

4 Tell the pairs to read out their dialogues. They should pay particular attention to the intonation.

5 Now ask the students to think of other clever, everyday inventions like stairs, doors, buttons, books, hammers and so on. They should go for simple examples, not high-tech inventions.

6 Round off the lesson by asking if anyone can think of anything that still needs to be invented. Are there any gaps in the market for goods or services that have yet to be filled? Note whether the students generally react positively or negatively to each other's ideas. The tendency to think positively or negatively can be discussed with the class, and their attention can be drawn to their thinking habits as the course progresses.

Service with a Smile (1)

Level
Intermediate

Time
45–60 minutes

Language Functions
Making and dealing with requests; asking for and supplying information

Materials
Small cards or pieces of paper

Before Class
Prepare the cards (see list of requests on page 27). You need one set per group of eight to twelve students.

In Class

1 Tell the class you want to talk about the concept of good service. Ask some of the following questions to set the scene:

- What words and expressions are associated with it?
- Can anyone relate examples of good or bad service from hotels, restaurants, shops, companies and so on?
- Can anyone tell the story of a complaint they made about goods or services and how it was dealt with?
- Is the customer always right?

2 Divide the class into groups of between eight and twelve students. Tell them they are to take turns at playing the part of the hotel receptionist in a large hotel. The receptionist should sit in front of the other students, if possible behind a desk. The other students will take turns to make requests.

Start with the ones written on the cards, but allow the students to provide their own examples if they spontaneously think of them. The receptionist should try to offer 'service with a smile' under all circumstances. This means being pleasant, polite, patient, practical, positive and professional, no matter how difficult the customers prove to be.

3 If necessary, quickly check through the language required. The customers will need to say, for example: 'I wonder if you could …', 'I'm afraid I've got a problem …' and 'Please do you think you could help me …' The receptionist needs to express helpfulness and cooperation. For example: 'Of course, Madam', 'Certainly, Sir', 'Is there anything else I can do for you?' and so on.

4 Have the first receptionist come to sit at the reception desk. Put the cards in a pile where the customers can reach them easily and let them take turns to come up and make one request. Each student in each group should get the chance to be the receptionist, and, if possible, every student should have one request for each receptionist. Keep the pace brisk. The requests should develop into a short exchange. Thus if a customer asks what the time is, the receptionist will tell them the time but also ask if there's anything else they need, and the customer might go on to ask where they can get a new battery for their watch.

5 Conclude the activity by asking: Who were the most professional receptionists? And who were the most difficult customers?

Service with a Smile (2)

Make a number of cards, each containing a request, message or query. These are the typical requests I use. Some of the cards spell out an instruction in detail. Others simply provide a prompt in a word or two.

- I can't remember my room number.
- Have you got a single room for me?
- How much is a double room with a shower and WC?
- Can I have breakfast in my room?
- Can you recommend a good restaurant?
- Is there an Internet connection in my room?
- Where can I buy an English magazine?
- There was a banana peel in the lift. My boss has fallen and sprained her ankle.
- I've lost my key.
- My credit card's stuck in the cash dispenser. Can you help me, please?

- What time does the conference start?
- Where can I park my car?
- Where can I post a letter?
- Can I change my room? I want a view of the sea.
- It says the restaurant is open until midnight, but it was already closed at 11.30.
- I've lost the charger for my mobile phone. Can you charge it for me?
- I'm all alone in town. It's my birthday. Will you have dinner with me tonight?
- Where can I leave my luggage?
- When do the shops open?
- I want to watch a DVD, and there's only a VHS video player in my room.

- Which tram do I need for the art gallery?
- Is there a public telephone in the hotel?
- My dog wants something to eat.
- I left my new briefcase with my laptop in it in the bar. Someone has taken it and left an old, empty one in its place.
- Is there a gift shop near the hotel? I want to buy some souvenirs.

- Where can I send a fax?
- How much does it cost to hire a car?
- Where can I buy stamps?
- The TV set in my room's broken.
- Where can I buy a telephone card?

- McDonald's
- hairdresser's
- Any messages?
- taxi
- Paracetamol
- Irish pub
- airport
- room with a shower
- chemist's
- travel agent's
- train station
- post office
- tourist information office
- toothbrush
- doctor
- dentist
- bus station
- English pub
- Chinese restaurant
- aspirin

- tickets for the rock concert
- tickets for the London Symphony Orchestra
- tickets for the pop festival
- tickets for the jazz concert
- tickets for Ajax vs Manchester United
- tickets for the Britney Spears concert
- tickets for the circus
- tickets for the cinema
- tickets for the darts tournament
- tickets for the snooker championships

Joyce and Ingrid

Level
Intermediate

Time
30–45 minutes

Language Functions
Solving problems; making recommendations

Materials
Copies of the worksheet

In Class

1 Tell the students you want them to focus on a problem concerning two secretaries in a large organization. Take the worksheet and half read, half describe the situation described there, adapting the language you use to the level of the class.

2 Give out the worksheet so the students can read the descriptions of the two secretaries' working styles.

3 Divide the class into pairs and tell them to discuss points on the worksheets.

4 Tell the students to report back on their conversations and let other students comment on the ideas that have been put forward.

5 Finish off with a vote. Who would rather have Joyce and who would prefer Ingrid as their secretary?

Joyce and Ingrid

**Read through the two texts describing the secretaries' working styles
and then discuss the questions with your partner.**

The first secretary, Joyce, is reliable, responsible and completes her tasks quickly and to a very high standard. She's been with the company for nearly three years. She's very efficient. But she takes various liberties. For example, when she has time, she reads books at her desk which have nothing to do with her job. She spends long periods on the Internet and sends innumerable personal e-mails. She often uses the photocopier to make copies which have nothing to do with the organization, and makes several short, personal phone calls on her mobile phone every day. Although she doesn't steal, small items of stationery do occasionally find their way into her handbag. She arrives at 8.30 on the dot and leaves at 5 p.m. sharp, or sometimes even a bit before. She thinks nothing of going against company policy if it suits her. She organizes her work well because she doesn't like working under pressure. She's a bit of a loner and doesn't show much interest in her colleagues' personal problems.

The second secretary, Ingrid, is nothing like Joyce. She works rather slowly, but comes in early and stays late so as not to get behind. She's been with the company for fifteen years and has a great deal of experience. She isn't very good with the computer, but is following an evening course at her own expense to improve. She's only just learning to use the Internet effectively and hardly ever uses the company e-mail system to send personal messages. She hasn't got her own mobile phone, so if she has to make a personal telephone call, she uses the company phone. She doesn't make many personal calls, but when she does, they're much longer calls than Joyce's. She never takes any stationery at all, nor does she make photocopies for herself. She's not as quick as Joyce, but she is very thorough and she works well under pressure. Ingrid is a sociable person and is very understanding if one of her colleagues has a personal problem.

- What is your immediate reaction to Joyce and to Ingrid?

- If you were their boss or the personnel manager, would you talk to Joyce about her behaviour?

- Would you say anything to Ingrid?

- Do you think they should both earn the same salary?

- If the organization were forced to fire one of the two secretaries, who do you think they should fire? Why?

- Who would you prefer as your secretary if you were a manager in their organization?

- If the managing director was looking for a secretary, would you recommend Joyce or Ingrid?

- What would you say if you were writing a reference for these two secretaries?

- If Joyce and Ingrid were to become managers after a number of years, which of the two would you rather have as your boss?

- Does your working style more closely resemble Joyce's or Ingrid's? Specify in which ways.

Talking Business in Class © Chris Sion published by DELTA PUBLISHING

AEAs: Abbreviations, Emoticons and Acronyms (1)

Level
Intermediate to Advanced

Time
15–30 minutes

Language Functions
Identifying the letters of the alphabet

Before Class
Prepare a list of abbreviations relevant to the needs and interests of the class.

In Class

1 Write the list of abbreviations one by one on the board asking the students to say what they stand for as you go. If the students can add a couple of their own, so much the better. The sort of abbreviations to use in a Business English class might also include a couple of general examples, or you might opt for a specialized selection directly appropriate to the students' backgrounds. A fairly typical upper-intermediate selection might read as follows:

CEO	RSI
MD	MBA
ETA	FOB
GM	CNN
WWW	VIP
FAQ	LCD
SMS	HTML
GPS	

2 Ask the students which letters of the alphabet are *not* in any of the abbreviations. This involves checking through the whole alphabet.

3 Divide the students into pairs. Tell them to write down their full names and check which letters of the alphabet are not included in them.

4 Check the results around the class. Which letters are not to be found in anybody's name?

5 Tell the students to work in pairs. They should make a list of some of the most frequent abbreviations they encounter at work and explain what they mean and their significance in their jobs.

6 Now ask the students if anyone knows how to 'smile in an e-mail'. Introduce them to the idea of emoticons and explain that an e-mail smile may be written like this :-). Point out that emoticons and acronyms are being increasingly used in e-mail and text messages. Moreover, the computer world is alive with acronyms. Ask if they use them themselves and if they know any others. Then quiz them on the examples in the list on page 31 and suggest that they send each other an e-mail or text message using some of this material before the next lesson.

7 Finish the lesson by asking if the students can relate any of the emoticons to their jobs. For example, a student might say of <:-) , the emoticon for 'stupid question', 'John Benson, my general manager, is a terrible listener and, as a result, is always asking stupid questions'.

NOTE: Two alternatives to using names in Step 3 are: the full name of organization they work for, or their e-mail address.

AEAs: Abbreviations, Emoticons and Acronyms (2)

Key to the abbreviations in Step 1

CEO	Chief Executive Officer	**RSI**	Repetitive Strain Injury
MD	Managing Director	**MBA**	Master of Business Administration
ETA	Estimated Time of Arrival	**FOB**	Free On Board
GM	Genetically Modified	**CNN**	Cable News Network
WWW	World Wide Web	**VIP**	Very Important Person
FAQ	Frequently Asked Question	**LCD**	Liquid Crystal Display
SMS	Short Message System	**HTML**	Hypertext Mark-up Language
GPS	Global Positioning System		

List of Emoticons and Acronyms

Emoticons (rotate the page right)

:-)	smile	**:-o**	amazed	**#-)**	What a night!
8-)	smile with glasses	**<:-o**	scared	**:-9**	Yum, yum!
:-{}	moustache and smile	**/-o**	bored	**@}->-**	a rose
:-{)}	moustache, beard and smile	**>-(**	angry	**=:-)**	punk
3:-o	cow	***#*!^*&:-)**	schizophrenic	**<:3)~~~**	mouse
:-D	laugh	**<:-)**	stupid question		
;-)	wink	**:-(**	sad		

Acronyms

2L8	too late	**B4**	before	**CUL**	see you later
4sale	for sale	**B4N**	bye for now	**FYI**	for your information
AAMOF	as a matter of fact	**BAK**	back at keyboard	**IC**	I see
ADN	any day now	**BAU**	business as usual	**IDK**	I don't know
AFAIK	as far as I know	**BBL**	be back later	**JK**	just kidding
AFK	away from keyboard	**BICBW**	but I could be wrong	**KIT**	keep in touch
AKA	also known as	**BQ**	beyond question	**L8R**	later
ASAP	as soon as possible	**BRB**	be right back	**TTYL**	talk to you later
BOGOF	buy one, get one free	**BTW**	by the way		

NOTE: Most of these emoticons and acronyms were taken from an article called *The WYSIWYG (what you see is what you get) Keypal Club* by Marcel Bittencourt Tavares in *English Teaching professional*, Issue 30, January 2004. If you want more examples, you can find lots of them on websites such as:

http://www.computeruser.com/resources/dictionary/emoticons.html

http://www.randomhouse.com/features/davebarry/emoticon.html

Creative Combinations

Level
  Intermediate

Time
  30–60 minutes

Language Functions
  Comparing information

Materials
  Overhead projector; blank transparency sheets; several sets of overhead-projector pens

In Class

1 Divide the class into pairs, with an A and a B in each pair. Give the As a blank transparency and an OHP pen and tell them to draw a grid of 16 squares (4 x 4) on their transparencies. The squares in the grid should be about 4cm x 4cm and should be numbered from one to sixteen. The numbers should be small enough for there to be space to write in the squares.

2 Now give the other students, the Bs, a transparency and an OHP pen. Tell them to place their transparency on top of their partner's (as an overlay) and trace the grid, so that they have a good, clear copy of it.

3 Tell the students to work individually and make a list of eight job-related topics. For example, A's list might include: personnel problems, job satisfaction, creative problem-solving, flexible working hours, logistics and so on. B might put down: time management, irritating colleagues, social benefits, corporate strategy, inefficient secretary and so on.

4 Tell the students that in each pair, A has the odd numbers and B has the even numbers. They should write their eight topics on their individual transparencies. In other words, A fills in squares 1, 3, 5, … 15 and B fills in 2, 4, 6, … 16.

5 The students should now overlay their two transparencies and relate sets of adjacent topics as discussion points. Thus if A has 'personnel problems' as point 1, and B has 'time management' as point 2, the pairs discuss 'personnel problems and time management'. They then go on to combine points 3 and 4, and so on.

6 Tell the students to come to the front (in pairs) and use the overhead projector to present their transparencies. They should focus on a couple of the most interesting pairs of points they discussed.

7 Finish the lesson by asking the students around the class to say which combinations they felt were the most productive.

NOTE: In Step 5, some combinations will inevitably generate more conversation than others. Tell the students to move on to the next one if they get stuck. If none of the adjacent numbers produce anything worth talking about, tell them to be flexible and look for any viable combinations from their lists. The aim is to facilitate conversation, not force it.

It Takes Two

Level
Intermediate

Time
20–30 minutes

Language Functions
Describing; expressing conditions

In Class

1 Ask the students if they know what a 'vicious circle' is, and introduce the idea of a vicious circle in a relationship. For example, the husband drinks because his wife nags him. She nags him because he drinks. Or the teacher is impatient because the students are restless. But the students get restless because the teacher is so impatient.

2 Draw a simple sketch of a man and a woman on the board. Tell students that the two people work together. Ask the students to suggest names for them and to supply other details such as their ages, nationalities, professions, the precise working relationship between them and so on.

3 Tell the students to think of some similar examples of what we might call 'behavioural vicious circles' in a business context. For example:

- He never asks her questions because she seems unwilling to share information.
  She seldom shares information because he never asks her questions.

- He's not very highly motivated because she never praises his work.
  She never praises his work because his motivation is so low.

- He shouts at her because she works slowly.
  She works slowly because she's afraid he's going to shout at her.

4 Ask whether anyone knows that the opposite of a vicious circle is a *virtuous* circle. Here, both people's behaviour is positive. For example:

- The manager trusts his staff and delegates important work to them which builds their confidence.
  The staff feel confident enough to take responsibility for the important work that has been delegated.

- The manager praises his secretary for her punctuality.
  She responds by continuing to be on time because this quality has been recognized and acknowledged.

5 For conversation practice, tell the class to discuss any cases of these sorts of behavioural vicious and virtuous circles from their own professional experience or everyday lives.

Learning Improvement

Date with a Dictionary

Level: Intermediate to Advanced

Time: 30–45 minutes

Language Functions: Comparing and contrasting

Materials: One monolingual English dictionary and one bilingual dictionary for each student

Aims: a) To develop awareness of the differences between English and the students' first language(s)

b) In general, to introduce the students to the experience of browsing through dictionaries

c) More specifically, to encourage the students to use monolingual dictionaries with a view to helping them to start thinking in English

Before Class: Ask the students to each bring a monolingual English dictionary and a bilingual dictionary to the next class; if possible, bring in a few dictionaries (monolingual and bilingual) yourself in case not all the students have them.

In Class

1 Tell the students to look through their notes and pick out between five and ten words or expressions they have translated into their own language. Tell them to check that the translations are correct by consulting a bilingual dictionary.

2 The students should now look up the words and expressions selected in Step 1 in a monolingual dictionary. Tell them to make notes so they can discuss the material later.

3 Ask the students to work in pairs and share their findings.

4 Continue with a whole-class discussion of any further interesting points that came up in the dictionary work. For example, one student might be taken by the innumerable uses of the verb 'to get' in English. Another might observe that the expression 'I'm pulling your leg' has the Spanish equivalent (literally translated) 'I'm taking your hair', while the corresponding German expression is 'I'm taking your arm'.

5 Finish with a general, open discussion of the pros and cons of translating. Some students might refer to words and expressions that are difficult if not impossible to translate and which have, in many cases, been assimilated into English, for example 'femme fatale', 'machismo' or 'Angst'.

Learning Sequences

Level: Intermediate to Advanced

Time: 30–45 minutes

Language Functions: Describing and comparing

Aim: To reflect on the most effective way to learn

In Class

1 Tell the students you want them to think about the best way they learn in general. Ask them to work individually and make a list as follows:

- things you have learned in the past;
- things you are learning now;
- things you want to learn in future.

Learning Improvement

At this stage, these lists should *not* include learning English. That only comes later.

2 Tell the students to work with a partner and spend a couple of minutes discussing the points they listed in Step 1.

3 Now tell the class to consider the skills they have mastered and the things they have succeeded in learning. After they have had a short while to think about it, ask them to work with their partners and discuss: How did they do it? How did they go about learning?

4 Tell the students to continue by focusing on one or two particular skills they have mastered. Tell them to draw a grid with five columns and trace their learning sequence. They should work step by step, from the point where they decided to learn to the point where they know they have mastered the skill in question. Take, for example, learning to swim:

5 Tell the students to talk about the stages of their learning sequences with their partner. In the course of discussing the examples, they should try to establish whether there are any patterns in their successful learning sequences. The point is for them to become aware of the most effective way for them to learn on the basis of their own experience.

6 Working individually, the students should now establish their learning sequence for English. They should then discuss with their partners how their English learning sequence compares with their successful learning sequences, and what could be done to improve the former by modelling it on the latter.

7 Finish the activity by telling the students to spend some time thinking about the activity over the next few days. On further reflection, they might come up with a new insight into the way they learn English which could help them learn more effectively. Encourage them to think back on the activity whenever they find something difficult to learn.

Step 1	Step 2	Step 3	Step 4	Step 5
I decide I'm going to learn to swim, find somewhere offering swimming lessons for adults and set the date to begin.	I watch other people swimming, both experienced and inexperienced, and concentrate on the way they move and breathe, particularly when they approach the water.	I buy a book about swimming (although I only read part of it).	I start swimming lessons and practise and practise and practise.	I know I've learned to swim because: • I don't sink! • I can get from one side of the pool to the other without touching the bottom; • I'm not nervous; • somebody asked *me* to teach her to swim!

NOTE: I learned the outline of this activity from Gene Early at a Neuro-Linguistic Programming (NLP) workshop.

3

Me and My Job

Work takes up a large proportion of our adult lives. Our jobs are intimately connected with our self-esteem and feeling of well-being. This section contains another set of job-related activities for the students to discuss, this time directly concerned with the students' own jobs. Being connected with the students' professional experience, they provide excellent starting points for getting them to open up and talk about their backgrounds in English. If some students don't have jobs, ask them about previous jobs they have had, holiday or part-time employment, or if necessary, to talk about the workplace of someone else they know, perhaps a parent or friend.

Working Diagrams

Level

Low Intermediate to Advanced

Time

45–60 minutes + several sessions of 20–30 minutes (see Step 4)

Language Functions

Presenting information; describing spatial relationships; asking and answering questions

Materials

Overhead projector, transparencies and overhead-projector pens; or flip chart with thick felt-tipped pens

In Class

1 Draw a rough diagram of your workplace on the board. This might be the room at home where you do your preparation or the department in the language school (or company) where you teach or both. Don't say what it is. Ask the students to guess what it represents, both in general and in detail. Prompt the students and elicit as much of the information as you can.

2 Use your diagram to talk about your job. What do you do? Who are the people you work with? Who is responsible to whom? What are their duties? How are their jobs connected with yours? Who do you like and dislike working with? Why? You can also include details about the physical environment you work in. For example, you can't open the windows because of the air conditioning, you're on the tenth floor with a beautiful view, and so on.

3 Tell the students you want them to draw their workplace and then present it to the class in the same way. One possible diagram might look like this:

reception	toilets	laboratory
secretary's office	large open office for 20 staff	conference room
storeroom	canteen	manager's office

Distribute overhead-projector pens and transparencies and tell the students they have about five minutes' preparation time. If you haven't got an overhead projector, use a flip chart. Tell the students not to go into too much detail – all they need is a rough sketch. Have them do a draft first if it helps them.

4 One by one, the students come to the front of the class, present their drawings and answer the other students' questions about their jobs. If necessary, ask a few questions yourself to get things started or keep them going. If there are a lot of questions, it is advisable not to do all the presentations in one lesson. Spread them out over a number of classes.

NOTE: Students might have to be resourceful in some cases. Thus a taxi driver might draw her car, or a person who works from home might sketch the living room. This doesn't matter. The sketches will still be a good starting point for job-related conversation.

The Heart of the Matter

Level
Elementary to Intermediate

Time
30 minutes

Language Functions
Expressing preferences and approval

In Class

1 Draw on the board a big letter 'I' followed by a heart on the board to indicate 'I love …'

2 Tell the students to contribute as many examples as they can of things that they love. Either let the students come to the front and write them on the board, or write them up yourself. Try to elicit a healthy variety of ideas, for example:

I love …
- my dog
- jogging
- reading
- gardening
- breakfast in bed
- pizza
- ice cream
- travelling
- my parents
- five-star hotels
- football
- my kids
- horror movies
- computer games
- poetry

3 Ask which of the items are job-related. Encourage both literal and metaphorical contributions; for example, 'The only time I ever stay in a five-star hotel is when I'm away on business', 'The way our warehouse is organized is like a horror movie', 'If my balance-sheet adds up right the first time I check it, it's like poetry' or 'I never have breakfast in bed during the week because I always leave for work before the rush hour'.

4 Clean the board and ask for as many similar but directly job-related examples as the students can think of. These should also be written up on the board.

I love …
- a clear desk
- reliable customers
- punctuality
- healthy profit margins
- increasing market shares
- new products
- state-of-the-art technology
- dealing with small organizations
- networking
- sociable colleagues
- realistic targets
- clear communication
- good technical service
- cooperation between departments
- a fair boss

5 Tell the students to work in pairs or small groups and discuss a selection of the examples listed on the board in Step 4.

My Work and I

Level

Intermediate to Advanced

Time

45–60 minutes

Language Functions

Describing; expressing preferences; presenting information

Materials

Small cards (about A5 size) of two different colours; pins and a pin board or similar system of displaying the cards; felt-tipped pens

In Class

1 Ask the students to each write two sentences, one containing the word 'work', the other containing the word 'life'. Tell them to read their sentences to the whole class and tell the students you want to talk about the relationship between life and work.

2 Give each student five cards (of one colour) and a felt-tipped pen. Tell them to write a couple of phrases connected with their jobs on each card. The phrases can refer to any aspect of their jobs, although obviously, the more interesting they are, the more stimulating the activity will be. Examples might include: working with people; my own boss; technically challenging; no responsibility; too much time on the road; competition with colleagues; no backing from management.

3 Now give them five cards of the other colour and tell them to write a couple of phrases connected with their personal values and world view on their cards; for example, always look on the bright side, nothing's impossible, honesty's the best policy, always expect the unexpected, beware of first impressions, seize the day, and so on.

4 Tell the students to work in pairs and discuss the points on their cards, particularly with regard to the relationship between their work and their world view.

5 Give the students five to ten minutes to prepare a short, informal presentation on the relationship between their work and their world view. They should use the cards to present the information from the front of the class.

Career Choices

Level
Intermediate to Advanced

Time
30–60 minutes

Language Functions
Describing and comparing

Materials
Copies of the worksheet

In Class

1 Go round the class, asking the students a selection of the following questions to lead into the subject of talking about their work. Be prepared to contribute a few details about your own background, but don't hog the conversation for yourself. Give everyone the chance to speak.

- What did/do your parents do for a living?

- Did you ever want to follow in their footsteps and do the same job?

- How did they react to the career you chose?

- As a child of various different ages, what did you want to be when you grew up?

- Did you/Do you ever visit your parents at their work?

- Did they/Do they ever visit you at work?

2 Divide the class into pairs. Distribute the worksheet and tell the students to discuss a selection of the points it contains. One pair might have a great deal to say about the professions of other members of their family. Another might want to focus on the things they like and dislike about their present job.

3 Conclude the activity by asking the students to report back on the most interesting, surprising or unusual aspect of what their partner had to say. Although intended to round the activity off, this step may actually open up many new opportunities for business conversation either in this or in subsequent lessons.

NOTE: Handle the question of the students' parents' professions tactfully, as your students may come from very different social backgrounds.

Career Choices

Part 1

Work with a partner and discuss a selection of the following points:

- What made you choose the profession you chose?
- Do you have any regrets?
- If you could have another profession today, what would you like to be?
- What do you like about your job today?
- What do you dislike in general?
- What specific points would you like to change?
- What other jobs have you done?
- What jobs have other members of your family done in the past?
- What jobs do other members of your family do at present?
- Do you know anybody else with an interesting job?
- What do you think you'll be doing professionally in ten years' time?
- If you could retire today on a reasonable pension, what would you do to fill your time?

Part 2

Fill in the form and then discuss it with your partner:

Professionally, I would rather do something:

■ technically orientated than care for people.	Yes ☐	No ☐
■ well paid but unsatisfying than satisfying but poorly paid.	Yes ☐	No ☐
■ practical than theoretical.	Yes ☐	No ☐
■ state-of-the-art than traditional.	Yes ☐	No ☐
■ in a small organization than a big organization.	Yes ☐	No ☐
■ with more computer contact than contact with people.	Yes ☐	No ☐
■ exciting but risky than steady and secure.	Yes ☐	No ☐
■ involving working for the state than in private enterprise.	Yes ☐	No ☐

Part 3

Write 100 words about what your job means to you (i.e. its importance in your life) and then share your thoughts with your partner.

Talking Shop

Level
  Intermediate to Advanced

Time
  45–60 minutes

Language Functions
  Exchanging information

Materials
  Copies of the worksheet

In Class

1 Ask the class if anyone knows the expression 'to talk shop' and explain that it means to talk about your job or profession, especially in a social situation. Ask if anyone has acquaintances who often talk shop and if any of the students often do so themselves.

2 Tell the students you would now like to give them the chance to talk shop in class. Divide them into pairs. If possible, they should share the same professional background and/or similar interests. Distribute the worksheet and tell the students to discuss some or all of the points listed on it.

3 Explain that the students should ignore any items that do not apply to their situation. Explain, too, that the items should be used as a springboard to open up conversation. The aspect of 'the last (time) ...' in some examples should not be taken literally. For example, if the last meeting they attended was uneventful but there was a particularly interesting one some weeks ago, the interesting meeting is the one to talk about.

Talk to your partner about some or all of the following points:

- the last time you used the Internet as a resource for something connected with your job.

- a recent presentation you gave (or attended) at work.

- a computer 'bug' you had at work in the last couple of weeks.

- an important memo, e-mail or fax you wrote (or read) in the last couple of weeks.

- a recent business letter you wrote (or received).

- the last business lunch you had.

- the last business meeting you attended.

- the last time you worked overtime or at the weekend.

- a recent business telephone call you made (or received).

- a recent trip in a company car.

- the last time you spoke to your boss.

- the last time you had 'one of those days' at work, a day when everything seemed to go wrong.

Talking Business in Class © Chris Sion published by DELTA PUBLISHING

You and Your Image

Level

Intermediate to Advanced

Time

30 minutes

Language Functions

Describing; expressing preferences

Materials

A selection of different bags (including a torn plastic one) and briefcases; a variety of extra items of clothing and other accessories; copies of the worksheet

Before Class

Put the materials in the classroom where they are concealed but accessible.

In Class

1 Tell the class you have a really special activity for them. Take the worksheets from an old, torn plastic bag. Don't distribute them yet. Then take a smart briefcase, put the worksheets in it, and repeat the lead-in to the activity exactly as you did before, this time taking the worksheets from the briefcase. Discuss the effect the plastic bag and the briefcase had on your image as a teacher and on the expectation of what sort of activity was coming.

2 Change some aspects of your appearance. For example, take off your tie, put on a hat, let down your hair, take off your watch and produce a very old clock instead and so on. Go on teaching (anything at all) and ask the students how your appearance affects your credibility.

3 Ask the class what other sorts of things you could change to alter your image. For example, you could be well groomed or scruffy; you could wear a lot of cheap jewellery, bleach your hair, and have a piercing or a prominent tattoo; you could take the register with a short stub of a pencil, a quill or with a gold pen. Try to ensure the examples are general points: this is not intended as a feedback session on your teaching.

4 Divide the class into pairs and distribute the worksheet. Tell the students to discuss a selection of points on it.

NOTE: This activity raises the question of the image of ourselves we are trying to create. In the course of the discussion, students will occasionally give each other suggestions about how they might improve their image. In doing so, they should be encouraged to be kind and constructive. Although potentially quite a probing awareness activity, 'You and Your Image' is not intended as an in-depth feedback session.

You and Your Image

Read through the worksheet. Then work with a partner and discuss a selection of the following points:

- What sort of image do you want to create at work?

- If you're on a business trip, does it make a difference if you use an expensive company car (or go first class if you travel by plane or train) and stay in an exclusive hotel?

- Would you feel comfortable buying a car you wanted but in a colour you hated if you could get it at a very good price?

- Would you buy an expensive designer watch rather than a simple classic one so you could show it off at work?

- Would you buy a piece of expensive designer clothing which didn't clearly display what make it was for other people to see?

- Are there any restaurants, pubs, clubs or cafés you visit because you feel they are 'the place to be'? Are there any others which you wouldn't visit under any circumstances?

- Is the part of the town where you live just right for you?

- Are you aware of other people's attempts to create a particular image of themselves in the workplace? What sort of image do the other people in your life try to create; for example, your colleagues, boss, business acquaintances, family, friends, neighbours and so on?

- What can you say about the image of your:
  - company?
  - department?
  - colleagues?
  - boss?

- Has your boss ever told you to improve your professional image, for example by clearing up your desk or paying more attention to your appearance?

What I'd Really Like to Know Is ...

Level
> Intermediate to Advanced

Time
> 30 minutes

Language Functions
> Asking and answering questions

In Class

1 Divide the class into pairs and tell them to talk about the organizations they work for. They should introduce the organizations to each other and should include both positive and negative aspects; for example:

- positive: highly successful multinational company, excellent social benefits for staff;

- negative: many manufacturing processes are not environmentally friendly, the head office is badly designed (sick building syndrome).

2 Now tell the students to work individually for a few minutes. Their task is to write five questions they would like to answer and five they would *not* like to answer about their organizations. The questions can refer to any aspects at all; for example, sales, profits, size, personnel, location, organization, benefits, unions, products, logistics, technical processes and so on.

3 Tell the students to work with their partners again. This time, their task is to compare their questions. Explain that it is not yet time to answer the questions. Before they do the answering, they should each add a few questions about their partner's organization to each other's lists.

4 Now tell them to take turns to ask and answer the combined set of questions on their lists.

5 Give the students a chance to report back on which questions they particularly didn't want to answer and why. How did they feel about these awkward, unwanted questions and how did they try to answer them?

Job Analysis

Level
Intermediate to Advanced

Time
45–60 minutes

Language Functions
Analysing; describing; asking and answering questions; persuading; expressing preferences

Materials
Small cards (about postcard size)

Before Class
Write one profession and a couple of skills required for that profession on each card. For example:

- dentist: gentle; able to bear others' pain
- firefighter: brave; cooperative (good at teamwork)
- postman: good at reading unclear handwriting; physically fit
- train driver: likes travelling; punctual

You need a classroom in which you can have several groups working in parallel and enough sets of cards for several groups of eight to twelve students.

In Class

1 Divide the class into groups of about eight to twelve students and give each group a set of cards, face down. Explain what's on the cards and read out a couple of examples. Then divide each group in half (As and Bs).

2 Have one student in each group turn up a card. This card might read:

doctor: good at working with people; caring; controlled emotions

The A students add to the list of skills a doctor needs; for example, must be willing to work long hours, if necessary on call 24 hours a day, a good listener, and so on. Meanwhile, the B students should brainstorm the job description for the job; for example, gives injections, prescribes medicines, stitches up wounds, and so on.

3 Tell the class that the next stage of the activity concerns a selection interview for a vacancy working in the profession on the card that has just been analyzed. The As are the candidates for the job and should each try to convince the Bs (the selection committee) that they would be the best choice. Give the As some time to prepare their arguments for employing them, and the Bs time to prepare the questions they should ask.

4 The Bs interview the As one by one. The As each state their arguments and try to persuade the Bs that they are the best candidate.

5 The Bs have a short meeting to reach a decision. While they do so, the As also meet and should also decide who gets the job. (They must now try to be professional and objective and should no longer push their own cases.)

6 The As and Bs now meet as one group and report back to each other on their decision. Once they have heard the other side's point of view, the As and Bs should argue it out further and try and reach a consensus as to who gets the job.

7 If there are several groups, get each group to report back on the interviews to the whole class.

8 Now tell the students to write down a couple of qualities that they need in their own jobs and give them a turn to say what these qualities are.

Muddling Through Meetings

Level
Intermediate to Advanced

Time
30–45 minutes

Language Functions
Making decisions; analysing; reporting

Materials
Copies of the worksheet

In Class

1 Lead into the subject of meetings by writing the following points on the board and asking the students to complete them, then read out what they have written.

When I have to go to a meeting …
During meetings …
After a meeting is finished …

2 Divide the class into groups of about five students. Tell them they have about fifteen minutes for a meeting. Their task is to decide on the following points to represent the nature of their group:

- a colour
- a number
- a letter of the alphabet
- a logo
- a slogan

3 Let the groups report back to the whole class on what they decided and why. As far as possible, let one student report on each point.

4 Now tell the class to pick a colour, number, letter, logo and slogan which represents the whole class. This might lead to quite lively exchanges as the more dominant students try to force their opinion on the others. Don't let it get out of control.

5 As a lead-in to the worksheet, ask how the simulated, rather chaotic meeting, in Step 4 compares with the sorts of meetings the students have to attend at work.

6 Divide the class into pairs and give out copies of the worksheet.

7 To finish off, tell the students to refer back to their statements in Step 1. Is there anything they could do to improve their attitude to meetings and their meeting skills?

NOTES: a) The instruction in Step 2 is intentionally vague. The aim of the activity is in part to see how consensus is reached in a group, even when the input is not altogether clear.

b) With a sophisticated class, appoint one student in each group to be the observer in Step 3 and then give the group members feedback on their behaviour in Step 4. The sort of points to look for are: Who was the most (and who the least) involved? Was the decision really a group decision, or did one student manage to force their will on the others?

Muddling Through Meetings

What generally happens at a typical meeting you have to attend at work? Read the worksheet, tick the boxes, then discuss your answers with a partner.

1 The agenda is:
   - distributed before the meeting. **Yes** ☐ **No** ☐
   - clear and to the point. **Yes** ☐ **No** ☐
   - followed strictly. **Yes** ☐ **No** ☐

2 Someone is asked to take the minutes.
   Yes ☐ **No** ☐

3 The chairperson talks too much and dominates the meeting.
   Yes ☐ **No** ☐

4 The chairperson allows other members to dominate the meeting so that quieter people, who might well have valuable contributions to make, are not given a chance.
   Yes ☐ **No** ☐

5 Native speakers of English do not try to use language that non-native speakers can easily understand.
   Yes ☐ **No** ☐

6 Time is not efficiently used, so too much time is spent on some topics and too little on others.
   Yes ☐ **No** ☐

7 Some people are allowed to 'score points' instead of addressing the real issues.
   Yes ☐ **No** ☐

8 Some people work to a 'hidden agenda' and are not open about their motives and ambitions.
   Yes ☐ **No** ☐

9 Decisions are taken too quickly.
   Yes ☐ **No** ☐

10 It is not always clear whether a decision has been taken at all.
   Yes ☐ **No** ☐

11 The conclusions are summarized and an action plan is usually drawn up to follow the meeting.
   Yes ☐ **No** ☐

12 People at meetings often feel their time has been wasted.
   Yes ☐ **No** ☐

NOTE: This worksheet is based on a similar one I developed with Martin Worth at the 3M Company. It in turn drew on *The Manager's Book of Checklists* by Derek Rowntree (Corgi Books).

Developing Small Talk

Level
Intermediate to Advanced

Time
45–60 minutes

Language Functions
Comparing and exchanging information

Materials
Lots of pictures cut from magazines (ideally pasted onto thin cardboard); copies of the worksheet

In Class

1 Showing a couple of pictures as prompts, ask the class what sort of things they talk about when they make small talk. Use the opportunity to exchange a few comments with the students about the news, weather, sports, the car, family matters, work and so on.

2 Divide the class into groups of about six and give each group about 25 pictures. Tell them to classify a few of the pictures into sets of two. These sets should depict opposites. Allow them to be as creative and flexible in their interpretations as they can. For example, a sports car in one picture and a piece of chewing gum in another might be used to illustrate 'expensive and cheap'; pictures of a North American Indian chief and an ant hill might be said to reflect 'management and staff'. The idea is to extend the range of subjects to talk about and gradually move on from small talk to other areas of discussion.

3 Ask each group to say what their best examples were. Suggest that they hold up the pictures if they are big enough to be seen by the whole class. If not, they should say what the pictures are in a couple of words. As they come up, write the paired sets of opposites on the board. The contributions might include examples such as the following:

- perfectionist or easy going
- morning or evening
- competitive or uncompetitive
- stressful or relaxing
- marketing or manufacturing
- active or passive
- low-tech or high-tech
- balanced or unbalanced
- team player or individual
- amateur or professional

4 Tell the students to work in pairs and relate the opposites on the board to their working lives. Even in the case of the examples which initially appear trivial, students will find associations with a little prompting and will invariably have interesting contributions to make.

5 As the next part of the lesson also requires pairwork, let people change partners if they want to. Then give out the worksheet and tell the class to discuss it.

Developing Small Talk

Here is a set of job-related points to talk about with a partner. As always, don't give one-word answers. Try to open up interesting conversations. It doesn't matter where the conversation leads to, as long as it's in English.

- What are your strengths and weaknesses professionally?

- Are you 'a different person' at home and at work?

- In the job you do, who do you most like working with (for example, your boss, secretary, colleague or customer)? Why?

- And who do you least like working with?

- Who would you like to change jobs with for a day?

- What would you not do at work for a million pounds?

- What is your strongest professional ambition?

- Give an example of a small thing you'd like to change that would make a big difference to your work.

- What is your pet hate in your workplace?

- Give an example of something you couldn't do without at work.

Talking Business in Class © Chris Sion published by DELTA PUBLISHING

Creative Revision 1

Remember to Forget to Remember

Level: Elementary to Advanced

Time: 20 minutes + 15 minutes in a later lesson

Language Functions: Remembering and forgetting

Aim: To actively revise vocabulary

In Class

1 Discuss with students how organizing vocabulary will help them learn it. Suggest that they divide the pages of their notebooks into sections so they can easily classify new vocabulary as they write it down. Discuss which categories they might want to choose; for example, 'very important', 'theoretical', 'just what I need', 'interesting but useless' and so on. Tell each student to select the categories that they feel will be the most useful. A page from one of their notebooks might look like this:

Interesting and/or useful	Not too easy to remember
Directly work-related	Indirectly work-related

2 Tell the students to look over some of their recent notes and divide the vocabulary into the categories they have chosen.

3 The next step is for the students to work in pairs and discuss and compare the vocabulary they have worked on in Step 2 in relation to the categories they have selected.

4 Tell the students to pick out from their notes about ten words or expressions they expect to *forget*. They should write them down on a list. Then tell them to share the contents of their list with their partners. Finally, ask them to bring the list to the next lesson.

5 In the next lesson, the students should again work with a partner, ideally with the same one they worked with in Step 4. They should each give the list of words they expected to forget to their partner. Now they should take turns to quiz each other on the list to see what they can recall, contrary to their expectations. In many cases, they will have learned the vocabulary. I tease them that they have forgotten to forget!

Creative Revision 1

Memory Aids

Level: Intermediate to Advanced

Time: 20 minutes

Language Functions: Revising vocabulary

Aim: To provide a useful method for vocabulary revision

In Class

1 Write ROY-G-BIV in large letters on the board and ask the students if they have any idea what it might mean. Let them ask questions and speculate for a while, then explain that it is a mnemonic, a memory aid. Any ideas what for? ROY-G-BIV tells you the first letters of the colours of the rainbow: Red, Orange, Yellow, Green, Blue, Indigo, Violet.

2 Ask the students if anybody uses any similar memory tricks to help them recall vocabulary and tell them you'd like them to develop some new possibilities. The idea is to remember just one or two words (or even clusters of letters) that will serve to trigger the vocabulary in question.

3 Tell the students to begin by looking at their notes and coursebooks and making a list of about twenty words they want to be able to remember.

4 Now ask them to think of whatever memory tricks they can to learn these twenty words. Some ideas are:

- use the first letters of the words to make a nonsense word like ROY-G-BIV;

- think of a word, then pair each of the letters of that word with one of the words you want to remember; for example, if you wanted to remember 'punctuality', 'interpreter' and 'negotiate', the first three letters would give you 'PIN';

- base the mnemonic on a set such as the four seasons or the days of the week.

5 Tell the students to actually try and learn the vocabulary selected in Step 3 using the methods devised in Step 4. Tell them to report back to the class on their progress at a later date.

NOTE: Point out to the students that there are no correct or incorrect mnemonics. The only important question is whether they are effective.

4

Bridging the Gap

One of the objectives of *Talking Business in Class* is for the students to shift their focus from carefully controlled interaction to spontaneously talking about their personal professional experience. Another objective is to shift the focus of attention from classroom situations to the real world. The activities in this section are included with this aim in mind.

Many of the activities in this section call on the students to find time for their English outside the classroom. Although professionals will invariably be under time pressure, they will understand that their progress will naturally be in proportion to the effort they make. Doing something for their English as an 'extra-mural activity' will facilitate effective learning, with the added bonus that it can be informative, fun and highly motivating.

My Territory

Level

Intermediate

Time

15–20 minutes

Language Functions

Giving and following directions

Materials

Street maps (see note)

In Class

1 Divide the class into pairs or small groups and give them the maps.

2 Tell the students to talk to each other about the places on the maps where they live, work or study. If possible, let them move round the room and look at several maps and show the details on their maps to a number of different students. They should refer to anything of interest and should use the opportunity to develop conversation. Here are two sample contributions of how the conversations may begin:

Eva This is the head office, where I work. Our technical support centre is over here, on the other side of town. It only takes five minutes to get there on the motorway. The warehouse is here. I don't have to go there very often. One of our key customers is building a new factory over here. One of our biggest competitors is just around the corner from them, so we've got to be very careful.

Frank Tell me something about the competitor.

Frank This is where I live. The college where I'm doing my computer course is over here. This is the route I follow to get to college. I cross the road over here and get the bus at the corner. Here's the swimming pool I go to on Sunday mornings. My girlfriend lives here now. She used to live on the other side of town.

Eva I stopped going to that swimming pool last year. Have you ever tried the one over here (*points to map*)? It's cheaper and less crowded.

NOTE: The maps required will depend on your teaching situation. You might have to ask the students in the previous lesson to help you by bringing local maps or maps of their home towns to class.

My Type of Word Processing

Level
Intermediate to Advanced

Time
30 minutes + 10 minutes in the next lesson

Language Functions
Reporting; comparing and evaluating

Materials
Copies of the worksheet; a typewriter (Step 1) and a computer (Step 5) are useful but not absolutely necessary

In Class

1 Bring a typewriter to the lesson. Demonstrate how it works. Let some students actually try it, particularly if some of the younger members of the class have never used one.

2 Ask around the class when, where and how the students learned to type and when they first used a computer for word processing.

3 Divide the class into pairs and tell them to discuss the following questions:

- To what extent do you use the computer for word processing at work?

- What do you think of MS Word? Are there any aspects of it you find particularly good and any others you find frustrating?

- Do you know any word-processing programs apart from MS Word, for instance LocoScript or WordPerfect?

- How do these various programs compare?

4 Stop the pairwork and ask if anybody knows the quick codes for MS Word; for example, what do you get if you press Crtl + A on a PC? ('Select all.') If you have a computer in the classroom, demonstrate the quick codes which are on the worksheet or let the students take turns at trying them out. If you haven't got a computer in class, explain the codes, letting the students guess them as you go.

5 Give out the worksheet so the students have it for reference. Ask if anyone knows any quick codes not included on the worksheet or has any other practical tips on using the computer that can be discussed in class.

6 Finish by suggesting that they try to find some more useful computer tips, for example from the Internet, and report back on them at the next lesson.

Ctrl + ...

N	new document	**F**	find	**M**	tab
O	open document	**G**	go to	**L**	left
S	save document	**H**	find and replace	**E**	centre
W	close document			**R**	right
P	print document	**Z**	undo typing		
		Y	repeat typing		
A	select all				
X	cut	**1**	single spacing		
C	copy	**2**	double spacing		
V	paste	**5**	1½ spacing		
B	**bold**	**D**	font options		
I	*italic*	**+**	superscript		
U	underline	**=**	subscript		

Note:
These commands are for PCs; for Macs, use the ⌘ key instead of Control.

Talking Business in Class © Chris Sion published by DELTA PUBLISHING

The Thief of Time

Level Intermediate **Time** 30 minutes + 30 minutes in the next lesson **Language Functions** Planning; comparing **Materials** Copies of the worksheet

In Class

1 Ask the students if they know the expression 'Procrastination is the thief of time'. Go on to elicit a comprehensive list of tasks they have to do before the next lesson and write them on the board. The list should be in as much detail as possible. You may use business-related or general items or a mixture. For example:

Job-related

- reserve meeting room
- register for conference
- ask secretary to book hotel room
- cancel sales training course
- buy secretary flowers for her birthday
- make appointment with manager
- top up paper in printer
- order office materials
- renew toner in photocopier
- attend to e-mail correspondence

General

- phone doctor
- cut grass
- make dentist's appointment
- fill up car
- change printer cartridge
- repair bike
- get film developed
- return video to Videotheque
- return books to library
- get hair cut

2 Give out the worksheet and tell the students to fill it in. They should use genuine tasks from their lives, even if these are not among the items on the board, and should prioritize them.

3 Divide the class into pairs and tell the students to compare their examples.

4 Tell the class you will ask them to report back at the next lesson on what they managed to do.

5 In the next lesson, ask the students to report back as mentioned in Step 4. This can be done in pairs, small groups or as a whole-class activity.

The Thief of Time

Fill in some of the tasks you have to do before the next lesson and mark them according to their priority. In other words, mark them on a scale from the most to the least important. Then discuss them with another student. Bring the worksheet to the next English lesson so that you can report back on you progress. How easily did you manage to do what you did? What stopped you from doing everything? Do you agree that 'Procrastination is the thief of time'?

Done ☐   Not done ☐   Half done ☐

Done ☐   Not done ☐   Half done ☐

Done ☐   Not done ☐   Half done ☐

Done ☐   Not done ☐   Half done ☐

Done ☐   Not done ☐   Half done ☐

Done ☐   Not done ☐   Half done ☐

Done ☐   Not done ☐   Half done ☐

Done ☐   Not done ☐   Half done ☐

Done ☐   Not done ☐   Half done ☐

Done ☐   Not done ☐   Half done ☐

Done ☐   Not done ☐   Half done ☐

Done ☐   Not done ☐   Half done ☐

Done ☐   Not done ☐   Half done ☐

Done ☐   Not done ☐   Half done ☐

Done ☐   Not done ☐   Half done ☐

Talking Business in Class © Chris Sion published by DELTA PUBLISHING

Points in Time

Level
Intermediate

Time
10 minutes + 20 minutes in the following lesson

Language Functions
Talking about the past

Materials
Copies of the worksheet

In Class

1 Introduce or revise the past continuous tense and give/elicit lots of simple examples: 'At 10 a.m. I was walking to the manager's office for a meeting,' 'At 12.30 I was writing a letter,' 'At 7 p.m. I was sitting in a traffic jam on my way home from work' and so on.

2 Give out the worksheets and tell the students they should fill them in the day before the next lesson. They need only make notes on the worksheets. It is not necessary to write whole sentences. In the next lesson, you will ask them to report back on what they had been doing at work the previous day at various times. Explain that they should try and find a range of examples. Even if they spent the whole day at a meeting, they should vary their contributions by including details such as making notes, asking a question, listening to a presentation, brainstorming, having a coffee break and so on.

3 In the next lesson, divide the class into pairs, and tell them to discuss and compare what they had been doing. The students might begin by practising 'controlled' examples of questions and answers such as, 'What were you doing at two o'clock yesterday afternoon?' 'At two o'clock I was talking on the phone'. Or they can make comparisons like 'While you were reading a book, I was doing my homework' or simply state what they were doing at a certain time.

4 They should then go on to use the material to develop informal conversations referring to their activities the previous day. As always, the simple examples described above should be used to generate as much business-related conversation as time allows.

NOTE: 'Points in Time' can easily be adapted to include an element of prediction in Step 2. In this case, the students first say what they expect to be doing at a particular time and then report back on what they actually did.

Points in Time

Fill in what you were doing at different times yesterday, beginning with the early morning. Try to get a good mix of activities; for example, talking to a customer, sending an e-mail, planning a trip, interviewing a candidate for a job and so on. You needn't write full sentences. Notes are sufficient.

What were you doing at these times yesterday?

7.00 _____

7.30 _____

8.00 _____

8.30 _____

9.00 _____

9.30 _____

10.00 _____

10.30 _____

11.00 _____

11.30 _____

12.00 _____

12.30 _____

1.00 _____

1.30 _____

2.00 _____

2.30 _____

3.00 _____

3.30 _____

4.00 _____

4.30 _____

5.00 _____

5.30 _____

6.00 _____

Talking Business in Class © Chris Sion published by DELTA PUBLISHING

And Now for Something Completely Different

Level
Intermediate

Time
15 minutes + several later sessions of
30 minutes each

Language Functions
Describing and explaining

Materials
A CD player and video (or DVD) equipment
might be needed in Step 5.

In Class

1 Tell the class you're tired of following the same basic pattern in your lesson. You want to try something new. In the next lesson, each student should come prepared, for example, to do the following three things: report on a minor newspaper item, ask a question and tell a joke. Taking these one by one, it's important that it should be a *minor* news item, or you'll find too many students coming with the same headline news. Set your own rules for the questions: they may be personal but not intimate or indiscreet. The jokes should not be vulgar, about ethnic or religious minorities or people who are handicapped. Depending on the class, you may also want to introduce a 'four-letter word' ban.

2 In the next lesson, divide the class into pairs or small groups and ask the students to report on their news items, ask their questions and tell their jokes.

3 Tell the students you want to think of some more, similar tasks for the next lesson. Either elicit the ideas from the students themselves or use the following list.

List of ideas

- computer tip
- problem or request for advice
- request for information
- interesting item found on the Internet
- recipe
- helpful hint
- item of useless information
- recommendations (restaurant, film, website, TV programme and so on)

4 Once again, the students report back on their tasks in the next class and you then set up the following three for the next lesson.

5 Once the ideas in Step 4 have been worked through, suggest that the students might like to bring in some of the following things to talk about:

- a 'knick-knack' or souvenir
- a game or puzzle
- an English CD or short video (or DVD) clip
- something home-made
- any other 'conversation piece'

NOTE: I have suggested using three items per lesson. However, you might prefer to just use one or two. Do what's most appropriate for you in the situation you're teaching in.

The Printed Word

<table>
<tr><td>

Level

Intermediate

Time

20–30 minutes + a later session of 30–45 minutes

Language Functions

Identifying objects; exchanging, comparing and analyzing information

</td></tr>
</table>

In Class

1 Tell the students to look round the class and identify as many instances as they can of printed matter; for example, books, brochures, covers of notebooks, slogans on T-shirts, posters, labels on bottles and so on.

2 If the examples in Step 1 are in English, discuss and explain the meanings. If they are in the students' first language, ask them to translate them into English and explain what they mean. If they are in any other, unknown languages, do your best to find out what they mean or just speculate about them.

3 Extend the search for instances of printed matter beyond the classroom. The list may now include items such as letterheads, timetables, tickets, theatre programmes, advertising hoardings, advertising on sports equipment, business cards, postage stamps, rubber stamps, shoe boxes, photocopies, labels on tins and bottles, CD sleeves, junk mail, computer print-outs, instruction manuals, leaflets, greetings cards, printed invitations and so on.

4 Tell the students you want them to bring some examples of printed matter to class to discuss at the next lesson. Texts should be in English if possible, but if you are not in an English-speaking country, they may bring something in their own language if they can't find anything else. In a class of a dozen students, you could ask each one to bring in two or three items. In a larger class, one item per student will be enough.

5 In the next lesson, tell the students to show what they have brought. Then divide them into small groups and tell them to explain and discuss the items and the language of the texts. Encourage the students to open up and develop simple, spontaneous, job-related conversations arising out of the printed matter. For instance, a student who has brought in a rubber stamp may describe the sorts of documents he/she has to stamp with it in the course of a day's work. A marketing person who brought in a glossy brochure from their company can talk about the products in it. Or someone who has brought in his/her mother's business card may have a lot to say about her job.

6 Round the activity off by asking round the class what the most interesting details of their discussions were.

Now That's What I Call Good Service!

Level

Intermediate to Advanced

Time

30–45 minutes + one later session of about 30 minutes

Language Functions

Analyzing qualities; investigating; exchanging and comparing information

Materials

Copies of the worksheet

In Class

1 Tell the class that the topic you want to talk about today is the quality of the service offered by various organizations; for example, companies, restaurants, shops, hotels, garages or government offices, to mention only a few. Spend a couple of minutes brainstorming key words and expressions associated with good service such as *polite, quick, helpful, attentive, professional* and so on.

2 Divide the class into pairs and ask the students to talk about instances of very good or very bad service from their own lives. One student may talk about an insurance claim which was quickly and efficiently handled. Another might have a story about difficulties she had with an airline when trying to change a booking.

3 Tell the students their next task is to discuss good service in their own organization. What is the company policy? How does the policy match up in practice? What are the difficulties they face in providing good service? How are complaints dealt with?

4 The next task is for them to think about the details that could be included on a form for assessing the quality of service offered by an organization.

5 Give out the worksheets and tell the students to compare their ideas with the points on the worksheet. They may add to or adapt the worksheet as they wish.

6 Tell the class that their homework is to use the worksheet to report back at the next lesson on a real experience they have in the next few days. They should pay attention to the service they receive in their everyday lives and then fill in the form with regard to one real encounter. For example, one student might report back on the service at the hotel he stayed in on a business trip; a second one refers to his treatment at the dentist's; another talks about the problems she came up against at the post office in tracing a parcel which had gone astray.

7 The students report back to the class in the next lesson.

Now That's What I Call Good Service!

Fill in this form with regard to an experience you have had, for example with a shop, government office, restaurant, doctor, business and so on. Focus on the service you received and make some notes about it. You will be asked to use your notes to report back to the class.

Date	Time
Place	
Organization	
Friendliness and politeness	
Helpfulness	
Willing to do 'that little bit extra'?	
Reliability	
Anything else?	
Did you feel good or bad after the encounter?	
Suggestions for improvement	
General impression as a rating on a ten-point scale (1 = very low; 10 = very high)	

Price Consciousness

Level

Intermediate

Time

20–30 minutes + a later session of 30–45 minutes

Language Functions

Reporting; investigating; comparing

Materials

Several everyday objects (see Step 1)

Before Class

Check that you know the exact prices of the items you use in Step 1.

In Class

1 Bring several small, everyday items into the class; for example, a packet of crisps, a calculator, some chewing gum, a roll of film, an airline ticket to New York and so on. You must know the exact prices of these articles.

2 Ask the students how much they think the items cost. This often generates a surprising amount of conversation; for example, 'I know where you can get it cheaper', 'In my country they're very expensive' or 'They've become much more expensive since we got the euro'.

3 Ask the students to discuss the following points, either in pairs or as a whole class:

● How price conscious are you: at home? at work?

● How price conscious are members of your immediate families?

● To what extent are/were your parents concerned with prices?

● What about at work? How price conscious is/are:
  – your company?
  – your boss?
  – your colleagues?

4 Tell the class that their task for next time is to investigate and then report back on the prices of various articles; for example, who can find the cheapest can of a particular beer? Who can find the cheapest airline ticket to Tokyo? How much is the latest computer software? The students may be content to get one price of an item or may prefer to compare prices of the same item at different shops. Comparisons may also be made using the websites that offer such services on the Internet. Another source of information is companies' price lists. Letting the students themselves decide what they want to investigate will itself generate a great deal of conversation.

5 The students report back in the next lesson.

NOTE: This simple activity is very productive. For example, the reference to parents in Step 3 might stimulate a self-made person to reflect on their childhood and the advantages their own children have today. The question of price consciousness is close to that of wastefulness, which is in turn associated with various environmental themes. Another issue which may arise in Step 4 is the question of quality and also whether 'cloned' products', that is, imitations, are as good as the originals. Price isn't everything.

Happy End

Level
Intermediate

Time
45–60 minutes

Language Functions
Narrating and discussing

Materials
Audio equipment with some gentle, relaxing music is useful but not essential.

Before Class
Adapt the story outline presented in Step 3 to the needs and interests of your class (see Note).

In Class

1 To warm the class up, ask if anyone has a favourite fairy story. What are the broad outlines of the best-known fairy stories? Which ones end happily?

2 Now tell the class you're going to ask them to be creative and write a story themselves. Divide the students into pairs or small groups. If you plan to use music, start it quietly in the background. Draw a simple sketch of a castle on the board, or let one of the students come up and draw one.

3 Tell the students that their task is to write a story centring on the castle (see Note). The stories needn't be written out in full. Notes are perfectly satisfactory. Their creations should contain the following ingredients:

- A person comes to the castle with a wish they want granted or in search of something that they very much desire.

- They are received by three different people in three different parts of the castle. First, at the entrance, by someone at the castle gate. Second, by someone inside the castle, perhaps in the grand hall or perhaps somewhere else. Third, by a person at the top of the tower.

- Neither of the first two people can grant the wish. The wish can only be granted at the top of the tower, and the story must have a happy end.

4 As you give them this input, build up the scene slowly. Tell them to imagine the castle, the surroundings and the interior. They should also include the people in the story, with a word about their characters and feelings. Encourage them to use whatever sounds and evocative images they can to make their stories interesting.

5 Give the students about twenty minutes to prepare. When they have finished, let them tell their stories to the class, who then express their reactions and discuss any issues raised, for example the importance of positive thinking and perseverance in business, and personal anecdotes paralleling the stories.

NOTE: Students will frequently refer the story to their own situations quite spontaneously. However, I generally encourage them to do so by incorporating more specific references into the input. For example, with a group of students training to be receptionists, I might say, 'There is a receptionist behind the counter in each of the three rooms in the castle.' One point that should then be dealt with in the discussion phase is the way the visitor was received. On an in-company course in the manufacturing industry, I might say, 'You can hear the rumble of machines in the castle cellar.' The reference to machines naturally leads the students to introduce a job-related element into their stories.

Creative Revision 2

Marketing Vocabulary

Level: Elementary to Advanced

Time: 30–40 minutes + a further 20–30 minutes if you do Step 5

Language Functions: Revising vocabulary

Aim: To provide a useful, amusing, business-related method for vocabulary revision

In Class

1 Tell the class to look through their notes and coursebooks and make a list of about a dozen words and phrases they want to revise.

2 Brainstorm a selection of typical forms of merchandising. Try to get as many ideas as possible, for example:

caps	T-shirts
socks	vests
underwear	pens
pencils	rubbers
notebooks	wrapping paper
labels	stickers
toothpaste	soap
bracelets	rings
football shirts	sky-writing
chewing gum	sweatbands

3 Divide the class into pairs or small groups. Tell them to use the vocabulary selected in Step 1 on the merchandising items in Step 2. Encourage them to be creative and to 'think big' when it comes to quantities. For example, 200,000 caps with the inscription 'I'm going home at five o'clock' (NOT 'going to home' or 'going at home'). Or 1,000,000 pencils with the slogan 'I'm looking forward to see**ing** you at the meeting' (NOT 'to **see** you'). If they want to draw simple illustrations of the products, so much the better. They should be prepared to present their product package to the class.

4 The students briefly present their ideas and show their illustrations (if they've done them) to the whole class.

5 Although this is intended as a Learner Training activity in the first instance, it could easily generate further business conversation topics, for example:

- Talk about merchandising in your company.

- At what point does merchandising become overdone?

- Can you see any potential for even more merchandising of a product or service anywhere, a gap in the merchandising market?

Creative Revision 2

Football Fantasy

> **Level:** Elementary to Advanced
>
> **Time:** 20–30 minutes
>
> **Language Functions:** Revising vocabulary; reporting
>
> **Materials:** An overhead projector with transparencies and overhead-projector pens
>
> **Aim:** To provide unusual associations for vocabulary revision

In Class

1 Ask the class if they can name the positions in a football team – for example, keeper, defender, mid-field player or striker – and draw (or let a student draw) a simple diagram of a team formation on the board.

2 Tell the students to look through their notes and coursebooks and to pick out at least eleven words, expressions or grammar points they want to revise.

3 Now tell the students to work in pairs. They should draw up an imaginary football team using the vocabulary they want to revise as the names of the players. If they wish, they may include five extra players as substitutes, and they should give their team a name. They may also include any other relevant details, particularly with business associations, for example transfer fees and sponsors. It may be a men's, women's or mixed team. An example of an intermediate mixed team would be as shown below.

4 Distribute the pens and transparencies and tell the students to copy their teams onto a transparency.

5 The students present their teams to the class. Tell them to comment on the teaching points they have selected; for example, the difference between 'loose' and 'lose', or that 'being late' is not the same as 'being *too* late', to take two points indicated in *The Management Tigers* team below.

TMT (*The Management Tigers*)

Joe <u>At</u> Home

Mia <u>Late</u> For Work (NOT Too Late For Work)	Bill <u>Sensitive</u> (NOT Sensible)	John <u>Raise</u> Your Salary (NOT Rise)	Pat L<u>oo</u>se

Fred Went <u>To</u> A Meeting   Laura Lie-Lay-<u>Lain</u>   Hilary Off Sick <u>For</u> A Week
(NOT Went In A Meeting)   (NOT Since)

Anna <u>Since</u> Four O'Clock

Adam <u>No</u>, Thank You   Maria <u>Typed</u> 100 Letters Last Week
(NOT Thank You)   (NOT Has Typed)

5

The Business of Thinking

No matter how much business people may enjoy talking about their jobs, there comes a moment when they want to go on to philosophize a little and engage their minds on other subjects. One's professional interests can't be completely separated from the rest of one's life. Mastering clear thinking and logical analysis, making value judgements, speculating on the nature of existence, and refining general communication skills are particularly challenging processes in another language. The activities in this section provide some stimulating classroom topics, which should result in a great deal of lively discussion.

A Little Logic

Level
Advanced

Time
20 minutes

Language Functions
Expressing logical connections;
drawing conclusions

In Class

1 Ask the students if they know what a syllogism is. Explain that it may be defined as an argument in three steps, with two linked examples leading to a 'proof'. One of the best known is:

All men are mortal.
Socrates is a man.
Therefore Socrates is mortal.

2 Discuss that the reasoning in a syllogism may be valid or invalid. Moreover, that the validity of the arguments is independent of the truth of the premises or the conclusion contained in the syllogism. The logic of the argument may be invalid, even though the three statements are all true. Discuss examples such as the following with the class.

- All bicycles have two wheels. A tandem is a bicycle. Therefore a tandem has two wheels. (valid)

- All bicycles have two wheels. A tandem has two wheels. Therefore a tandem is a bicycle. (invalid)

- All managers drive company cars. Kim is a manager. Therefore Kim drives a company car. (valid)

- All managers drive company cars. Kim drives a company car. Therefore Kim is a manager. (invalid)

3 Check both the truth of the propositions and the validity of the arguments with the class. Frustration and confusion may well result, making for a really lively discussion.

4 Divide the class into pairs. Tell them to write a couple of syllogisms which are job-related, then decide whether their syllogisms are valid.

5 Students take turns to read out their syllogisms. The rest of the class should listen carefully and say whether they think the arguments presented in the syllogisms are valid or not. Interesting topics used in the syllogisms may be discussed immediately or used as material for later conversation classes.

NOTE: Point out that you can falsify any statement beginning with 'All ...' by finding just one counter example. Take the statement 'All politicians are dishonest all the time'. If you can find an instance of just one politician who is honest on one occasion, the statement is false.

Contradictions

Level

Intermediate to Advanced

Time

45–60 minutes

Language Functions

Expressing logical connections;
drawing conclusions

Materials

Small cards (about postcard size)

Before Class

Prepare a list of statements like those in
Step 4, each written on a small card.

In Class

1 Read the students a few statements from the
following list and ask them to specify what the
contradictions are. Encourage the students to
develop these points in discussion, wherever they
lead.

- This morning, I went to a meeting after lunch.
- I didn't sleep a wink last night. I had a terrible
  nightmare.
- She kicked me with her hand.
- It's boiling cold.
- I'm going to write an e-mail yesterday.
- I'm too tired to go to sleep.
- I've seen it so often I don't know what it looks
  like.
- She lost control carefully.
- I can see what you're doing there behind my
  back.
- Don't open your mouth when you talk to me.
- I only take risks in business if I know I'm going
  to be successful.
- I can see what you're thinking.

2 Tell the class to work in pairs and spend a couple
of minutes brainstorming contradictions in the

world of business; for example, a factory claiming
to make home-made products or a slow express
service. Then have the students read out these
business contradictions to the whole class, again
letting them argue freely about them.

3 Building on the statement in Step 1, 'I can see
what you're thinking', move the discussion on to
consider that there can also be a contradiction
between our verbal and non-verbal
communication. We might say, 'I understand' or
'I'm not angry' in such a way that our body
language clearly contradicts our verbal statement.

4 Give the students (one by one) a card with one of
the following statements written on it. They
should read the statement 'incongruently', that is
as if they don't really mean it. Their body
language and tone of voice should contradict the
content of the statement.

- You're very well informed.
- This is the best company in the world.
- It's really simple.
- That product sounds interesting.
- I am concentrating.
- Of course I understand.
- It's amazing.
- Luckily we have Ms Taylor here today.
- It doesn't matter.
- It's not a problem.
- I am listening.
- I am looking.

5 Finally, ask the students if they know people
whose behaviour is frequently incongruent. Tell
them to keep an eye open for incongruity in
future, particularly in business situations such as
negotiations. They'll also find plenty of examples
by observing sales people push their products, to
say nothing of watching politicians on television.

NOTE: I got the germ of this idea from my daughter,
Katya.

Paradoxes

Level
Intermediate to Advanced

Time
30 minutes

Language Functions
Expressing possibility, impossibility
and necessity

In Class

1 Explain to the class that a paradox is a seeming contradiction, an unusual or surprising statement that goes against expectation; for example, a salesman who says, 'All salesmen always lie.' This seems quite simple at first sight: but isn't it impossible? If the salesman's statement is true, it is not so that 'All salesmen always lie' because the salesman is telling the truth in this case. On the other hand, if the salesman's statement is false, we must conclude that some salesmen do sometimes tell the truth! This modern version of a classical paradox can yield a great deal of conversation.

2 Ask the students if they can think of any paradoxes, and discuss them if they can.

3 Write up a selection of the following paradoxes on the board, eliciting as much of the material as you can and encouraging the students to add lots of examples of their own:

- A secretary who can't keep secrets

- An expensive way of saving money

- An uncompetitive competitor

- An improvised marketing strategy

- An inconvenient way of saving time

- An inefficient efficiency expert

- An unauthoritative director

- An indecisive decision-maker

- An unbusinesslike business person

- An unprofessional professional

- A wasteful means of saving energy

- A forgetful memory trainer

4 Divide the class into pairs and tell them to discuss the paradoxes listed in Step 3. Are they apparent contradictions or real contradictions?

NOTE: I consulted Nicholas Falletta's book *The Paradoxicon* (Turnstone Press) in developing this activity. I can recommend it if you want some background about paradoxes.

Silence is Golden

Level

Upper Intermediate to Advanced

Time

30–60 minutes

Language Functions

Asking questions; clarifying and interpreting body language

Materials

A video camera, TV monitor and video recorder make a wonderful supplement to this activity, although they are not absolutely essential.

In Class

1 Brainstorm with the class all the ways they can think of for asking for silence, for example:

Sssshh!
Shut up!
Please be quiet.
Please!
Ladies and gentlemen, …
Can we have a little less noise, please?
Good morning.
This is an important point.
Listen!
You may not believe this, …

Putting finger to lips
Holding up hand as a gesture to stop
Knocking on desk
Clapping hands
Simply standing and waiting
Eye contact
Coughing
Cupping hand to ear to indicate 'I can't hear you'

2 Tell the class you want to talk about silence. Point out that silence is actually a means of communication. As the psychologist Paul Watzlawick says, 'It is not possible to not communicate.' We communicate all the time via body language: by our gestures, eye contact, facial expression and so on. Elicit from the class that silence may express any of the statements below. Wherever possible, get the students to demonstrate these messages silently.

- I (don't) understand.
- I'm (not) interested.
- Leave me alone.
- Please ask me.
- I've got nothing to say.
- I'm confused.
- I don't dare to contribute.
- I'm depressed.
- I'm homesick.
- I'm in another world.
- I'm (not) thinking about it.
- I'm thinking about something else.
- I'm worried.
- I'm (not) concentrating.
- I'm tired.
- I'm afraid.
- I'm dreaming.
- I'm in love.
- I don't want to be impolite.
- I don't want to talk about that.

Silence is Golden

3 Tell the class you are going to ask one student to come to the front to be in the 'hot seat'. The other students should ask him/her questions. He or she must remain silent and should not say anything. Tell the class they have about ten minutes to prepare their questions. The questions may be about anything at all, although obviously you are likely to get more interesting reactions if the questions are a little provocative or controversial. A good mixture of questions is best, for example: Do you like your boss? Do you think you should be allowed to listen to the radio at work? Imagine you had to condense all next week's work into one day: how would you feel? Would you like to spend next Sunday playing golf with your co-workers? Did you hear that your computer's been infected by a new virus and that you've lost everything? Do you like sitting there? Do you think these questions are interesting? Why don't you say anything?

4 Ask for a volunteer to come to the front and sit in the hot seat, facing the class. Tell them how to respond as follows:

Option A
The student at the front should react silently to the questions, but should express answers and reactions to the questions intentionally; for example, by shrugging their shoulders, nodding or shaking their head and so on.

Option B
The student at the front should try not to react to the questions at all. The rest of the class should try to (gently) provoke a reaction.

5 The students now ask their questions and the student at the front responds silently. Video the interaction if you can.

6 Discuss what the silences expressed. Compare what the members of the class thought the student at the front was expressing with what he or she wanted to express. It is fascinating to refer to the video if you have been able to film the activity.

7 Give a couple of other students the chance to be in the hot seat and silently react to some questions. Another possibility is to have two or three students at a time at the front so you can compare their silent behaviour.

8 Conclude the lesson with a discussion of some or all of the following points. All the examples may be related to a professional context.

- When is it advisable to keep silent?

- And when is it necessary to speak one's mind?

- What effect does other people's silence have on you?

- Do you find it easy to remain silent?

- Have you ever spoken out and later wished you had remained silent?

- Have you ever remained silent and then later wished you had spoken out?

Some of My Best Friends Are Extraterrestrials

Level

Intermediate to Advanced

Time

30–45 minutes

Language Functions

Making suggestions; expressing opinions; making moral choices; expressing conditions

Materials

Copies of the worksheet

In Class

1 Ask the students if they believe in extraterrestrial beings, flying saucers and life elsewhere in the universe.

2 Continue to build up the activity by asking them to express their 'gut reactions' to aliens in one sentence.

3 Now tell the class you've just heard the most amazing news and ask them to speculate what it might be. Tell them that some aliens from another planet have landed in town! What do they think the alien beings might look like? Spend a couple of minutes encouraging the students' imaginations to flow. Get them to draw some simple sketches which can be shown round the class or drawn on the board.

4 A news flash has just been received. There are aliens here in the building! What should we do? Get some quick responses around the class.

5 Divide the class into pairs and give out copies of the worksheet.

6 Finish off by asking the students to report back briefly on the most interesting aspects of their paired discussions.

NOTE: This seemingly innocuous activity can touch students quite deeply. At one level, it's good fun. At another, it impinges on our attitudes to greed and exploitation, 'them' and 'us', humanity and inhumanity. In my experience, students tend to have strong convictions about the whole question of extraterrestrial life.

Some of My Best Friends Are Extraterrestrials

Discuss a selection of the following points with your partner:

- If alien beings came down to Earth, should we try and make friends with them?

- How should we treat them if they are hostile? Should we attempt to capture them?

- Would you be prepared to invite extraterrestrials into your home?

- Would you accept them marrying into your family?

- If they wanted work, what sort of job would suggest for them? Blue collar? White collar? Managerial?

- What business prospects might aliens offer, for example partners in intergalactic trade?

- There would probably be a lot of money to be made from keeping them in a zoo, but would this be acceptable?

- There might be a lot of money to be made from serving them as a delicacy in a restaurant. How do you feel about eating alien meat?

- Another business venture might be using their skin for belts, bags and shoes. What would the prospects be? Could we breed them? Is there an ethical issue?

- Could we use alien beings instead of animals for medical research, work on genetic modification and for experiments in the cosmetics industry?

Talking Business in Class © Chris Sion published by DELTA PUBLISHING

What a Piece of Work!

Level
  Intermediate to Advanced

Time
  45–60 minutes

Language Functions
  Describing and comparing

In Class

1 Introduce the topic either by referring to a quotation such as Hamlet's famous cry, 'What a piece of work is man!' or making a provocative statement such as 'Most animals are far more human than human beings!'

2 Explain that you want to talk about 'What makes human beings human?' Write a few ideas up on the board and encourage the students to add ideas of their own. For example:

- speech
- some animals might work, but they don't do business
- freedom
- ethics
- reason
- responsible for our actions
- self-control
- walks upright
- controlled use of fire
- cooked food
- highly developed use of tools
- belief in a higher being
- works for money

- artefacts
- creative
- sex not simply for reproduction
- names
- compassion
- laughter
- clothes

3 Divide the students into pairs and tell them to discuss the ideas on the board and any other relevant ones that might occur to them. Tell them to include in their discussions any relevant business-related aspects. Set a time limit of about 30 minutes.

4 When the class comes back together, go through a selection of items on the list on the board, giving the students the chance to report back on their discussions. There is so much to say that, in my experience, the students will still sometimes be talking about the topic long after the lesson is over.

NOTE: Be sure not to alienate the women in your class by constantly referring to 'men'. Rather refer to 'people', 'mankind' or 'human beings'.

Quotable Quotes

Level

Intermediate to Advanced

Time

30 minutes + 30 minutes optional continuation (either in the same lesson or in a following one) + 20 minutes (if you choose to do Step 4)

Language Functions

Citing and explaining

Materials

Copies of a dictionary of quotations

Before Class

Collect a few of your own favourite quotations to share with the class and ask the students to bring a couple of their own favourite quotations to the next lesson.

In Class

1 Tell the class a couple of your favourite quotations, preferably writing them on the board to give the students a chance to think about them.

2 Ask the students to tell the class some of the quotations you asked them to prepare (see 'Before class' above). First, let them read their quotations and then have them to come up to the board and write them down. Encourage the students to comment on the quotations, explain why they chose them and answer any questions. As always, the more conversation that can be sparked off, the better.

3 When the board is full, tell the students to work in pairs and discuss the quotations. Which do they most and least agree with? Do the quotations match their experience? Can they relate them to their work as well as their lives in general? Do they understand them all? Can they explain them? How would they explain them to a child? Which do they think is the best? Why?

4 A further continuation is to ask the students to bring examples of quotations from sources such as the following to the next English class as the basis of discussion:

- a business letter
- a product label
- a memo
- a brochure or leaflet
- an e-mail
- a conversation at work
- a fax
- a business lunch
- a presentation
- the minutes of a meeting

Mind Your Own Business!

Level

Intermediate to Advanced

Time

30 minutes

Language Functions

Reported speech; expressing opinions and preferences; making moral choices; expressing conditions

Materials

Copies of the worksheet

In Class

1 As the class if they know what a 'telltale' is, and explain if they don't that it is similar to a spy or informant, someone who reveals information about other people which those people would probably prefer kept confidential. Tell them today's activity concerns the moral question of when to tell and when not to tell. We might well despise a telltale, but when to tell is not always as clear cut as it seems.

2 Ask the class to discuss the following case with a partner and report back to the group:

When she goes for a job interview, Jane Morrison is surprised to see her old school friend, Sandra Harris, is the receptionist. While she's waiting, Jane confides to Sandra that she's pregnant. Should Sandra pass this information on to the selection committee?

3 Hand out the worksheets and tell the students to discuss the issues presented there with a partner. Encourage the students to add further situations of their own. Tell them they are also free to add any personal experiences, be they the ones who told tales or the ones who were told on.

4 Tell the students to report back on their discussions. It might be of interest to draw up a table on the board on which to record the number of students in favour of telling and not telling for each of the issues.

Mind Your Own Business!

Read the worksheet, tick the boxes, then discuss the following situations with your partner.
When should you tell and when should you not tell employers, the authorities or the police?
When is it necessary to tell on someone, even if it is none of your business? Is there a difference
between confiding in a friend about what another person has done and 'telling tales' about them?

- Marion reads the paper at work when the boss is out.
  Tell ☐ **Don't tell** ☐

- Denise is sitting in a corner of the cafeteria crying.
  Tell ☐ **Don't tell** ☐

- Mervyn has a stiletto knife in his briefcase.
  Tell ☐ **Don't tell** ☐

- Pete and Petra were smoking in a non-smoking area.
  Tell ☐ **Don't tell** ☐

- Sammy and Sally were smoking marijuana in the car park in the lunch break.
  Tell ☐ **Don't tell** ☐

- Eric and Erica were kissing in the conference room.
  Tell ☐ **Don't tell** ☐

- Florence and Lawrence were making love in the warehouse.
  Tell ☐ **Don't tell** ☐

- Fred has an alcohol problem: he even drinks at work.
  Tell ☐ **Don't tell** ☐

- Tina helps herself freely to office stationery supplies.
  Tell ☐ **Don't tell** ☐

- Christine has made five copies of her son's thesis (1,000 pages each) on the company photocopier.
  Tell ☐ **Don't tell** ☐

- I know my next-door neighbour has a job, even though she draws unemployment benefit.
  Tell ☐ **Don't tell** ☐

- Harry is a truck driver. He drives far longer hours than the law allows.
  Tell ☐ **Don't tell** ☐

Talking Business in Class © Chris Sion published by DELTA PUBLISHING

Talking about Time

Level	
Intermediate to Advanced	
Time	
30–45 minutes	
Language Functions	
Exchanging information; expressing preferences	
Materials	
Copies of the worksheet	

In Class

1 Begin by asking the class what the time is. Expect as many different answers as there are students.

2 Tell the students to show each other their watches and compare them. (The watches themselves, not just the time.)

3 Tell the students to estimate the time between two signals. For example, snap your fingers, wait for a given number of seconds and then snap your fingers a second time. How long was the interval between the two snaps?

4 Tell the class that today's topic is 'Talking about Time'. What is time? Why is it so difficult to talk about it, even though we all know exactly what it is?

5 Ask the class to think of as many words and expressions connected with time as they can and write them up on the board, for example:

punctual, early, late, on time, just in time, deadline, second, minute, hour, day, week, month, year, unpunctual, watch, stopwatch, time switch, clock, tick-tock, bell, alarm, moment, instant, period, date, postdate, tempo, duration, calendar, schedule

6 Give out the worksheets and tell the students to discuss them in pairs. If the students manage to use any of the words on the board in discussing their worksheets, so much the better.

Talking about Time

Discuss the following points with your partner.

- How many clocks and watches have you got at home and at work? Where are they? Include your computer, fax machine, mobile phone and so on.

- Which of your clocks or watches is your favourite?

- Do you try to set your clocks and watches accurately?

- Can you remember your first watch and the first time you wore it?

- Do you prefer a digital watch or clock, or a conventional, analogue one (with hands)?

- Do you use an alarm clock or radio alarm to wake up in the morning? If so, what time is it set for?

- Do you find it easy to get up when it goes off?

- Are you a punctual person, both at work and socially?

- Do you expect other people to be punctual? Do you have higher expectations in professional situations?

- Do you plan journeys, both business trips and others, so that you have a healthy margin to catch your plane (or bus or train or whatever), or do you usually arrive just in the nick of time?

- When you travel on business, have you ever missed (or nearly missed) an important connection by plane, bus or train?

- How important is time to you at work and in everyday life? Have you got any ideas on the best way to organize your time; for example, making a list of things to do today, deciding which are the most important, and then planning how much time you want to spend on them?

- It is a well-known saying in business that 'time is money'. Do you agree?

Talking Business in Class © Chris Sion published by DELTA PUBLISHING

Learning, Language and Identity

Split Personality

Level: Advanced

Time: 45–60 minutes

Language Functions: Describing and comparing

Materials: Audio equipment and some relaxing background music is useful but not essential.

Aims: To develop awareness of the nature of English compared to the students' first language(s) with particular reference to personality factors and individual thinking styles

In Class

1 Tell the students you want to compare the experience of speaking their own language with speaking English. Tell them to think of a subject to work on. This could be anything from discussing a controversial issue to trying to solve a problem or telling a story. Make sure everyone has found something and help any students who find it difficult.

2 Tell the students to work alone and spend a few minutes quietly talking to themselves about the subject they have chosen *in their own language*. Let the students stand up, move round the class or even go for a short walk if your teaching situation permits. Playing some peaceful background music should help to set the right mood.

3 Now tell the students to repeat what they talked about in Step 2, but this time talking to themselves *in English*. Steps 2 and 3 require about five minutes each.

4 Tell the students to work in pairs and discuss what they talked to themselves about in Steps 2 and 3. They should also compare the experience of talking English and their own language. If they aren't aware of all the following points immediately, tell them to try and observe themselves over the next few days.

- Can they describe in general terms what it feels like to talk English?

- How do they sit, stand and move when talking English?

- How do they hold their heads?

- How do they move their eyes?

- Do they have different mental pictures when talking English?

- Do they think differently in English?

- Do they have different personalities in the different languages?

5 Give the students the chance to report back to the whole class if they wish.

NOTE: Supplementary material may be found in my books *Talking to Yourself in English* (Training Etcetera) (Book 1: Intermediate ISBN 90-74645-01-1; Book 2: Advanced ISBN 90-74645-02-X).

Learning, Language and Identity

Personality Awareness

Level: Advanced

Time: 30–45 minutes

Language Functions: Expressing opinions; describing; comparing

Aims: To develop awareness of the nature of English compared to the students' first language(s) and of individual personality factors which might influence the learning process

In Class

1 Collect a short list of discussion topics on the board. Some may be your own input, others may be elicited from the class. The activity works best with controversial topics. Formulate the topics provocatively, for example:

- All employees should be paid the same wage, as they all play an indispensable part in company business.

- 'Inside information' is confidential and should never be discussed with unauthorized parties, either inside or outside the company.

- Smokers should be guaranteed the right to smoke at their workplace.

- Secretaries should be seen and not heard.

- As long as you've got a job, it doesn't matter what your company produces or how it does so.

2 Divide the class into pairs of students who speak the same language. For example, in a multilingual class, you might have pairs of Japanese, Arabic or Spanish speakers working together. In a monolingual class, simply pair the students. Their task is to discuss one (or more) of the selected topics *in their own language*. Give them no more than ten minutes for this stage.

3 The pairs should now discuss the same topics again, this time *in English*. Tell the students to compare the experience of discussing the topics in different languages. What language problems did they have? Did they have any difficulties apart from language problems? Do we to some extent become another person in speaking another language?

4 Finish off by letting the students report back to the whole group on significant similarities between their languages and English and on any personality differences they noticed when speaking the two languages.

NOTE: I don't know if there are research findings on personality differences when speaking different languages. Students and acquaintances of mine report that differences do exist; for example, some people find it easier to express anger or swear in English as opposed to their own first language, because for them English is not restricted by the taboos associated with their upbringing.

6

Presentations

Having the students give a talk to the class, typically about their hobbies, home countries, holidays or jobs, is traditional teaching fare. The talks are frequently supplemented by question time, making the lesson an excellent means of generating conversation. *Talking Business in Class* sets out to give these talks a professional finish.

The presentations you set should depend on the level, experience and interests of your class. Many people find addressing an audience from the front of the room an extremely harrowing experience, let alone in a foreign language. The better prepared the students are, the more confident they will be. Give them whatever help they need. It is often worth letting them run through their presentations with a partner before they give them from the front of the class.

Be tactful and constructive when you give feedback. Always ask the speakers how they themselves would evaluate their own talks. Be generous with your praise and encouragement. If you want to improve your students' performance, remember that one compliment is more effective than a thousand critical comments, no matter how well meaning. Identifying details such as 'you twitched' or 'your hands were trembling' is not likely to make the student less anxious next time.

Think carefully about the order the students should present in. Is it best to choose the more outgoing students first? Or do the quiet ones want to get the ordeal over with quickly? Discuss this with the class and respond to their requests wherever possible. Note that in setting up a round of presentations, it is always advisable to arrange to have one or two students as stand-bys for each lesson in case the student whose turn it is cannot do their presentation as planned.

No Need to Be Nervous

Level
Intermediate to Advanced

Time
45 minutes + two later sessions of 30 minutes

Language Functions
Describing and explaining; asking and answering questions

Materials
Small cards or slips of paper (about postcard size)

In Class

1 Give each student three cards and explain that you want to help them to cope with their 'public-speaking nerves'. This activity will help them learn to think on their feet.

2 Tell the students to think of three interesting aspects of their jobs they would like to talk about; for example: (dis)advantages of new personnel policy for sales people, introduction of flexible working hours, possible takeover by a multinational, cultural differences in the department, latest technical developments in a product line. They should write *one* of these aspects on each of their cards.

3 Divide the class into pairs. Tell them they have fifteen minutes to discuss the points on their cards. It is important that they discuss *all* the points on both sets of three cards. This means they have about two minutes for each point.

4 Tell them to write their names on each of their cards. Collect one card from each student, then a second card, then a third card, so that you have three separate sets of cards with each set having one idea from each student. Take one set of cards, shuffle them and explain that you are now going to turn up the cards one by one and ask the student whose card comes up to talk about the subject on the card for one minute.

5 Turn up the first card, let the student speak about the subject. Allow a couple of questions, then proceed to the next student.

6 Tell the students that you will use the second set of cards in the same way in the next class and the third set in the class after that.

NOTE: The fact that the students have already discussed their topics in pairs means that even though they don't know when they will be called on in Step 5, they are prepared. Of course, they may still get nervous while waiting, but the preparation they did in Step 3 should help them find the confidence they need.

Effective Presentations

Level
Intermediate to Advanced

Time
30–45 minutes + several sessions of 30–45 minutes in later lessons

Language Functions
Presenting information; evaluating

Materials
Copies of the worksheet (you need one copy per student per presentation, spread over a number of sessions)

In Class

1 Tell the students to work in pairs and discuss the following points:

- Presentations you have attended in the past, attend today and will attend in the future.

- Presentations you have given in the past, that you have to give in your present position and that you will have to give in the future.

- The best presentation you ever attended.

- The worst presentation you ever attended.

2 Tell the students to report back to the whole class so that you have an idea of their experience of attending presentations given by other speakers and of making presentations themselves.

3 The students should again work in pairs. If there are significant differences in their experience of presentations, try to pair experienced with less experienced students. If possible, avoid having two students with very little or no experience of presentations working together. Tell the pairs to discuss: 'What makes a presentation effective?' Give them about ten minutes for this stage and

tell them to make a few notes so they can report back to the whole class.

4 When they report back, ask each student to contribute one point to begin with so that everyone gets a chance to say something. Then, once you have been round the whole class, you can ask for additional comments from whoever might have them. The students should explain their points, and the class should discuss them as they come up. Write them on the board and supplement them if important aspects have been overlooked.

5 Tell the class you will be asking them to take turns to give a five-minute presentation on an interesting aspect of their jobs over the next few lessons and that you want to give them a checklist to use to analyze the presentations. Give out the worksheet and allow time for the students to read and discuss it. Are there any points on the checklist which were overlooked in the discussion in Step 4? Did any points come up in Step 4 which are not included in the checklist?

6 Make a timetable so that the students know when their turn is and give them some time to think about which subjects they will present.

7 The students give their presentations in the next lessons. Copies of the checklist should be distributed for each presentation, and the class should fill in their comments. Perhaps ask individual students to focus on particular points on the checklist. It is very important that after the presentations, once the questions have been answered, the speakers are given a chance to say what they thought of their own presentation. Each presentation should then be analyzed using the checklist. Combine your own impressions with those of the class. Stress that the comments should be as helpful, practical and constructive as possible.

What Makes a Presentation Effective?
Checklist

1 STRUCTURE

- Was there a clear beginning, middle (the main part) and conclusion?

2 TIME

- How long was the whole presentation?
- How long were the beginning, middle and conclusion, taken separately?
- How long was question time?

3 AUDIO-VISUAL AIDS

- Could everybody hear?
- Could everybody see?
- Were the audio-visual aids clear, helpful and a useful support for the speaker's message?
- Did the overhead projector, computer and video (or whatever other equipment) function as required?

4 SPEAKER'S VOICE

- Loud enough?
- Clear enough?
- Varied enough?
- Pleasant intonation or dull monotone?

5 CONTENT & COMPREHENSIBILITY

- What exactly did the speaker want to say?
- Was the speaker clear about what they wanted to say?

- Did the speaker take the audience's professional background into account?
- Did the speaker use 'meta-comments', that is, refer to what they were going to say and guide the audience with statements such as: 'There are three main aspects' or 'Now that we've finished the introduction, we can move on to the really important point'?
- Did the speaker use any jokes or gimmicks to get the audience's attention and, if so, were they effective?

6 BODY LANGUAGE & RAPPORT WITH THE GROUP

- Eye contact established and maintained with the whole audience?
- Posture (style of standing, sitting or moving)?
- Movements of hands and feet?
- Were the body language and the voice in harmony? In other words, did the speaker look and sound as if they believed their own message?

7 QUESTION TIME

- How were the questions asked and how were they answered?
- Why did/didn't you ask questions?

8 ACCURACY OF THE LANGUAGE USED

(You might need to take a separate page for this.)

Talking Business in Class © Chris Sion published by DELTA PUBLISHING

Be Prepared

Level

    Elementary to Advanced

Time

    45 minutes + a later session of 30–45 minutes

Language Functions

    Presenting information and opinions; giving and receiving criticism

Materials

    Copies of the worksheet

In Class

1 Tell the students that, as part of their course, you will be asking each of them to do a short presentation. Ask them one by one what they feel about having to come to the front and talk to the class. Tell them that many people find it a strain to speak in public, even in their own language, but that the key to giving an effective presentation lies in the preparation.

2 Now explain that a critical element in the preparation is deciding not only what you are going to say but also what you are *not* going to say. Tell them to be strict on themselves in deciding what to omit. Further important points are: to be clear about just what it is that you want to say; to have a good, clear starting point to attract the audience's attention; and to leave your message ringing in the audience's ears at the end. These points are all referred to in the worksheet.

3 Tell the students you want them to prepare a two-minute talk. The topic is: 'Something important in your life (professional or personal)'. They have about fifteen minutes. Tell them not to worry, they won't have to perform in front of the whole class today, but will get the chance to practise it with a partner.

4 Give out the worksheets and tell the students to start their preparation. Check that everybody has been able to think of a subject.

5 When the fifteen minutes are up, tell the students to work in pairs and take turns to run through the rough drafts of what they want to say. They should give each other feedback and help each other improve their presentations. They should come away with a clear list of points to improve.

6 Set a timetable of when the students will give their presentations.

7 Tell the students that they should continue their preparation at home. Tell them that they should prepare, as it were, passively and actively. Passive preparation means mainly reading, writing and thinking. Active preparation means actually practising. It is a vital ingredient in preparing a lively talk. Recommend that the students practise delivering their talks to themselves and/or to friends or members of their family.

8 The students give their presentations at the next session.

NOTE: Although the example of the two-minute talk is used here, this approach to preparing a presentation can be used for any presentation.

Be Prepared

The content

In my presentation I am going to say ...	In my presentation I am not going to say ...

What is at the heart of what you want to say? Sum up your message in a maximum of 30 words:

What I want to say is:

The beginning

My first words are going to be:

The end

The message I want ringing in the audience's ears at the end is:

Portrait of the Group

Level
Elementary to Advanced

Time
45–60 minutes

Language Functions
Asking and answering questions; making notes; comparing and presenting information

Materials
Small cards; overhead projector with blank transparencies and overhead-projector pens

Before Class
Prepare a set of small cards. Each card contains one subject such as those listed below.

- Who works the most hours per week?
- Who sends and/or receives the most e-mails per day?
- Who has the most powerful computer?
- Whose telephone bill is the highest/lowest?
- Who has the most and who the fewest books?
- Whose department is the largest/smallest?
- Whose home is the largest/smallest?
- Who has the most and who has the fewest brothers and sisters?
- Who commutes the longest distance to work?
- Who went to bed latest last night and who got up earliest this morning?
- Who drives the biggest, fastest, newest car, and who the smallest, slowest, oldest one?
- Who works for the largest company?
- Who has the most and who the fewest pairs of shoes?
- Who has been working for their organization the longest?
- Who has the most CDs, DVDs and/or videos?

In Class

1 Give each student one of the cards you prepared (see 'Before class'). Tell them you will give them fifteen minutes to interview the other members of the class. They should write down the information they gather, as their next task will be to present the information to the group. Students who aren't satisfied with the subject on their card may exchange it with a classmate or choose another suitable subject themselves.

2 After the fifteen-minute interview period, give the students some overhead-projector transparencies and pens and tell them to analyze the data they have collected. They should then prepare a transparency showing the information they have gathered as part of their presentation. The presentation should not be longer than three minutes, and the students should generally be allowed no more than one transparency each. Tell them to plan it carefully. It is advisable to do a rough draft on paper first.

3 Discuss the order of the presentations with the class and make a timetable so that all the students are clear about when it is their turn.

4 The round of presentations begins. One by one, the students come up to the front and present the information on their transparencies. Allow questions and comments at the end of each presentation. Apart from learning something about each other, you should find a great deal to discuss. The transparencies will probably vary considerably. Some will show bar charts, others pie charts, others a sketch or a few words summing up the conclusion. Yet another point to talk about is which transparencies showed the information most effectively.

Demonstrations

Level
Intermediate to Advanced

Time
30 minutes + several subsequent sessions of 25–30 minutes

Language Functions
Describing and explaining; asking and answering questions; expressing conditionals

Materials
A variety of devices that can be demonstrated

In Class

1 Bring in an everyday device, gadget or appliance, such as an electric razor or radio-alarm clock, and demonstrate how it works. Tell the students to ask you lots of questions and write some prompts on the board to get them going. For example:

- What is this button for?
- What happens if you turn this knob?
- What does the display show?
- What does this switch control?

2 Tell the students you want them to do some demonstrations and discuss with them who wants to demonstrate what. Examples of suitable appliances are: calculator, camera, video camera, laptop computer, digital wristwatch, mobile phone and so on. Make a schedule of forthcoming lessons and plan who is going to demonstrate what when. Tell them that the demonstrations should last between five and ten minutes, and that they should be prepared to answer questions.

3 The students give their demonstrations over the next few lessons, as arranged in Step 2.

4 An optional follow-up is to repeat the activity using old-fashioned appliances. Suitable examples would be: adding machine, typewriter, box camera, clockwork alarm clock or spirit duplicator. Explore your grandparents' attic to look for something old and interesting to demonstrate!

5 Tell the students you want to set up a second round of demonstrations, this time using old-fashioned appliances. Make another schedule as described in Step 2. Bear in mind that the students will need some time to look for things to present. It might be necessary to bring in some old appliances yourself for those students who haven't managed to find anything, or ask other members of the class if they can help.

6 The students give their second demonstrations over the next few lessons as scheduled.

Reporting Back

Level

Intermediate

Time

30 minutes + several further sessions of 10–20 minutes

Language Functions

Gathering and reporting information; note-taking; asking and answering questions

Materials

Overhead projector with transparencies and overhead-projector pens and/or large sheets of flip-chart paper with thick felt-tipped pens

In Class

1 Tell the students you want to give them practice in giving short presentations about different aspects of their (working) lives. You are going to give them a task and ask them to report back to the class over the next few lessons. Explain that they should gather the data carefully, and ask them to take the activity seriously. The presentations should not be longer than five minutes.

2 Discuss the following topics with the class and get each student to pick one topic. It doesn't matter if several students select the same topic. The students may decide on the time frame they are reporting back about, which might be a week, a weekend or a month. Make a note of the topics chosen, and fix the dates when the students will report back. Give the materials to the students who will be reporting back at the next class and encourage them to use them in presenting their information.

- Number of meetings attended
- Number of e-mails received
- Customers visited
- Approximate number of calories consumed
- Physical exercise
- Hours of overtime worked
- Hours of sleep
- Time spent with family
- Number of cigarettes smoked
- Quantities of beverages drunk
- Time spent surfing the Internet
- Hours of TV watched
- Telephone calls made
- Letters sent and received
- Amount of junk mail received
- Miles driven, including business trips

Note that the definition of the task can itself generate a great deal of conversation. If a student has to report back on how much junk food they have eaten during the week, there could be some lively exchanges about just what 'junk food' is. The 'miles driven' example might generate discussion of the number of kilometres there are in a mile. Don't hesitate to add to the list or adapt the items to your class's special interests.

3 At subsequent sessions, the students report back on the topics they have selected and answer any questions. Use the occasion as a springboard to generate as much conversation on the various topics as you can.

Magic Potion

Level
Intermediate to Advanced

Time
30–60 minutes + several later sessions of
15–30 minutes (see Step 5)

Language Functions
Presenting information

Materials
Overhead projector with transparencies and
overhead-projector pens and/or large sheets of
flip-chart paper with thick felt-tipped pens

In Class

1 Ask the students if they would be prepared to take
a language-learning drug to improve their
learning ability. Expect some lively exchanges
here. Some students may feel that the use of any
drugs is immoral except for medicinal purposes.
Others may accept the notion of a learning drug
only if it were cheap and without side effects.
There may also be some students who feel that
learning is only worthwhile if it involves effort.

2 Put on your most convincing and mysterious
voice and tell the students that while visiting the
Medieval Library of Child Psychology, you came
across a reference to an ancient magic learning
potion. Unfortunately, the precise instructions
have been lost.

3 Divide the class into pairs and tell them to think
up an imaginary magic language-learning potion.
Their task will be to present their idea to the
class. The presentations should be no longer than
three minutes. The sorts of points to mention are
ingredients, taste, side effects, dosage and price.
The students should also include imaginary
references to sales figures, marketing strategy,
technical details or any other business-related
aspects they can. They should also give the
potion a name.

4 Distribute the materials and set a time limit – say
ten minutes – for the preparation. The pairs may
decide whether they want to share the task of
presenting or not. Leave it up to them, but make
sure that the more assertive students aren't
bulldozing the quieter ones against their will.

5 The students present their ideas. Be sure to allow
some time for questions and for discussion of the
merits of the various potions at the end of each
presentation. Depending on the size of your class,
you may have to spread the activity over a
number of sessions.

NOTE: Thanks to my students, Kerstin G., Jutta S. and
Mike E. for the germ of this activity.

professional *perspectives*

professional perspectives is a series of practical methodology books designed to provide teachers of English with fresh insights, innovative ideas and original classroom materials.

Other titles in the series include:

Creating Conversation in Class
by Chris Sion
More than 100 imaginative ideas and stimulating activities designed to get students talking in class

Humanising your Coursebook
by Mario Rinvolucri
A wide range of activities designed to extend typical coursebook language practice by engaging students creatively and productively

The MINIMAX Teacher
by Jon Taylor
Practical, easy-to-use activities that generate the maximum student output from the minimum teacher input

Using the Mother Tongue
by Sheelagh Deller and Mario Rinvolucri
Ready-to-use activities which make creative use of the students' mother tongue in the language learning classroom

The *Resourceful* English Teacher
by Jonathan Chandler and Mark Stone
A complete teaching companion containing 200 classroom activities for use in a wide range of teaching situations

For a full list and further details of titles in the *professional perspectives* series, contact the publishers at:

DELTA PUBLISHING
39 Alexandra Road
Addlestone
Surrey KT15 2PQ

Tel +44 (0)1932 854776
Fax +44 (0)1932 849528
E-mail info@deltapublishing.co.uk
Web www.deltapublishing.co.uk